Q의 의미

Q의 의미

이 제 영

도서출판 시간의물레

Contents

1. 이제 Q 방법론을 이해하자 ‖ 7
2. Q 방법론의 개요 ‖ 14
3. Q-Methodology Analysis의 의미와 평가 ‖ 18
4. 스티븐슨과 Q 이론 ‖ 31
   1) 유희이론의 적용 ‖ 31
   2) 주관성과 객관성의 종합 ‖ 32
   3) 양자이론(Quantum Theory)의 적용 ‖ 35

5. Q 방법론의 이론적 배경과 적용 ‖ 40
   1) 소개 ‖ 40
   2) Q 방법론의 발전적 역사 ‖ 41
   3) Q 방법론의 이론적 배경 ‖ 43
   4) Q 방법론과 전통적 방법론과의 차이 ‖ 46
   5) Q 방법론의 효용과 실용성 ‖ 49
   6) Q 방법론에 대한 인식분석 ‖ 52
   7) Q 방법론에 대한 비판적 분석 ‖ 56
   8) Q 방법론의 기여와 발전 ‖ 62

Contents

 6. Q 방법론의 역사와 원리 : 심리학과 사회과학 ‖ 65

 7. 주관성과 커뮤니케이션 ‖ 78

 8. Q 방법론의 설계 ‖ 89

 9. Q 방법론의 적용과 이해 ‖ 96

10. Q와 R의 차이점과 장단점 ‖ 103

11. 맺음말 : Q의 연구 및 발전 방향 ‖ 109

◐ 부록 ‖ 113

1. Q-sort instructions for any Q-sample ‖ 114

2. Brown summarizes the comparisons he makes between Q and R methodologies, further underscoring their methodological differences. ‖ 128

1. 이제 Q 방법론을 이해하자!

이 세상의 다양한 이슈와 의견, 주제 등에 관한 유형화 연구를 위해 채택한 Q 방법론은 William Stephenson에 의해 창안된 것으로서 그 동안 과학에서 무시되어 왔던 인간의 주관적 영역, 예를 들어 태도, 신념, 확신, 가치 등을 객관적으로 측정하는 방법론이라 할 수 있다. Q 방법론은 인간의 태도와 행동을 연구하기 위해 철학적, 심리학적, 통계적 그리고 심리측정과 관련된 개념을 통합한 방법론으로서 인간의 주관성을 정량적으로 분석할 수 있는 특수한 통계기법이다. 소비자의 인식, 가치, 태도, 신념과 같은 개념을 객관적으로 연구할 수 있는 방법으로서 가설생성을 위한 탐색적 연구와 이론의 검증과 같은 확인적 연구에서도 적용될 수 있다. 많은 수의 표본을 대상으로 한 횡단적 특성을 지닌 R 방법론에 비하여 개인이나 소집단에 대한 깊이 있는 탐구가 가능하다는 점에서 소비자 행동 연구에 유용성이 매우 높다.

인식론적 관점에서 볼 때, Q 방법론의 가장 큰 특성은 발견적 추론(abduction)에 근거를 두고 있다. Peirce에 의하면, 과학적 탐구의 세 단계는 발견적 추론(abduction), 연역(deduction), 그리고 귀납(induction)의 순으로 이루어지며, 과학적 지식을 얻는 방법은 연역에 의해 명제와 결과 사이의 논리적이고 입증할 수 있는 가설을 설정하고 귀납에 의해 경험적인 검증을 통해 가설을 확립하는 단계를 거친다. 그러나 연역은 가설의 필연적인 귀결을 전개할 뿐이며, 귀납은 어떤가를 알아보기 위한 자료의 분류에 지나지 않으므로 현상을 이해하려면 발견적 추론에 의해야 한다(김홍규, 1990; Abduction Homepage, 1999).

Q 방법론의 발견적 추론의 특성은 가설생성의 논리를 뒷받침하고 있으며, 과학적 발견으로서의 새로운 길을 열어주고 있다. 이상과 같은 발견적이고 탐색적인 특성과

더불어 Q 방법론이 갖는 또 하나의 중요한 특성은 개인의 주관성에 본질을 두고 있는 과학적 접근방법이라는 점이다. Q 방법론은 '외부로부터 설명'하는 방법이 아니라, '내부로부터 이해'하는 접근방법이며, 이것은 연구자의 가정에서 출발하는 R 방법론과는 달리, 행위자인 응답자가 스스로 그들의 의견과 의미를 만들어 가는 자결적 정의(operant definition)의 개념을 연구자가 조작적 정의(operational definition)로 채택하고 있는 가장 중요한 근거가 된다(김홍규, 1994). 이러한 방법이 과학적이라는 의미는 체계적이고 객관적인 방법을 적용한다는 의미이며, 구체적으로는 요인분석이란 통계적 방법을 사용하는 것이다. R 방법에서의 요인분석은 변수를 요인화하는 반면, Q방법에서는 사람을 요인화하는 것이다. 그러나 두 방법의 차이가 단순히 변인과 사람을 전치시키는 것이 아니라, 개인 간에 차이가 있는 인간의 특성(Variables of a Transindi- vidual Character)의 관점에서 개인의 고유한 가치준거의 관점으로 전환하는 것이다(Brown, 1995). 이러한 인간의 주관성에 관한 객관적인 방법론이라는 Q 방법론의 독특성은 자아심리학의 영향을 받았으며, 이것은 소비자연구에의 적용가능성을 시사하고 있다.

소비자는 저마다 자신의 주관에 대한 표현방식과 객체에 대한 지각상태가 상이하다. 또한 동일한 객체나 상태에 대해서도 자신의 준거에 비추어 지각하고 판단하며, 의사소통방식에 따라서도 달리 표현할 수 있다. 그러므로 이러한 소비자 개인의 주관성을 기존의 객관적인 접근방법을 통해 연구하는 데에는 한계가 있으며, 객관성이 결여된 접근방법 또한 과학적 접근법으로서 문제가 된다. 따라서 주관성에 대한 객관적인 접근방법인 Q 방법론(Brown, 1996)을 이용함으로써 개인의 주관성을 바탕으로 한 소비자의 태도와 행동에 대한 과학적인 접근을 할 수 있는 것이다. 객관주의 심리학의 측정도구가 자아의 표면 수준을 측정하는 것이라면, Q 방법론은 한 개인의 잠재적 행위인 주관적 자아를 측정하는 방법으로 고안된 것이다. 그 동안 소비자의 인지와 태도 및 행동에 대한 많은 연구들은 대부분 자아의 표면적인 수준만을 측정하고 있기 때문에 소비자에 내재되어 있는 자신을 근거로 한 '나'라기보다는 관찰자의 관점에서 본 '표면적인 나'를 다루는 것이어서 소비자의 개성과 행동의 차이를 가져오는 내면적인 주관성에 대한 깊은 이해를 하기가 어려웠다.

Q 방법론은 주관성을 과학적으로 측정하는데 효용이 있다. 인간의 주관성은 입증하기 쉽지 않지만, 주관성은 일정한 구조와 형태를 띠고 있다. 연구를 위하여 주관성의 구조와 형태를 측정하는 데에 Q 방법론의 효용성이 있다.[1] 또한 이 연구방법은 주관성의 과학화에 기초를 제공한 일종의 철학적, 심리적, 통계적, 그리고 계량심리적 도구이다. Q 방법론의 우수한 장점은 인간행위의 주관적인 면, 즉 인간의 주관성의 관찰과 측정에 있다. 주관성이라 함은 동적인 상황 속에서 자결적(Operantly)으로 정의되는 개인의 관점 및 관념을 말한다.[2]

---

[1] Brown, S.(1980). Political Subjectivity : Applications of Q Methodology. New Haven: Yale University Press. 참조
[2] 김순은(1997). "지방자치의 발전을 저해하는 요인분석: Q 방법론의

따라서 Q 방법론은 그 동안 표면적인 소비자 특성 연구에 치중해 온 소비자 행동분야의 공백을 메우는 데 큰 공헌을 할 수 있을 것이다. 특히 앞서 선행연구를 통해 살펴본 브랜드 이미지 또는 개성에 관한 연구에서 발견된 각각의 유형이 요인분석에 의한 R 방법론에 의한 것으로 소비자의 주관적 자아를 간과하고 있다는 제한점을 해결할 수 있다는 점에서 의의가 있다.

이에 저자는 지난 15년 넘게 학술대회와 학회지를 통해 발표해온 경험을 통하여, 'Q'의 진정한 의미와 이를 통한 해석방향, '주관성'과 '객관성'연구의 차별적 특성을 논의하는 중요한 자리를 제공하는 첫 장을 마련하고자 한다.

한마디로, Q는 어느 한 방안 구석에 손전등을 비췄을 때, 전체를 파악하고자 하는 '가설생성'방식에 가깝고, R은 이러한 '가설생성'을 좀 더 '일반화'라는 여건의 확립을 위해 적용하는 '가설검증(영가설/연구가설)'으로 분류하여 이해할 수 있다.

적용". 〈정책분석평가학회보〉. 7(1). p.6.

이제는 "Q를 제대로 이해하고, 논의하는 자리를 만들자!"라는 명제를 공언할 시기가 온 것이 아닌가 싶다.

2016년 12월
강릉의 연구실에서
東陵 이제영

2. Q 방법론의 개요

    Q 방법론은 1953년 윌리엄 스티븐슨[William Stephenson (1902~1989)]의 'The Study of Behavior : Q-Technique and Its Methodology'의 출간으로부터 시작된다. 그렇지만, Q 방법론이란 말이 최초로 활용된 것은 1935년 윌리엄 스티븐슨이 Nature誌에 기고한 글인 'Technique of factor analysis'에서였다.[3]

    'The Study of Behavior'는 두 부분으로 구성되어 있다. 제 1부는 Q서론(prolegomenon to Q), 의존적 요인분석 (dependency factor analysis), R과 Q의 차이(Differentiation of R and Q), 표본과 구조(samples and structure), 심리학적 원리(psychological principles), 몇 가지 통계적·실험적 원리

---

3) 백용덕(1999). Q 방법론의 이론과 실제. 인하대학교 출판부. p.3.

(some examples) 등을 다루고 있다. 제 2부는 유형 심리학에의 적용(application to type psychology), 질문지의 사전분석(the prior analysis of questionnaire), Q 방법론과 자아심리학(Q Methodology and self psychology), Q 방법론과 인성(Q methodology and personality), Q 기법론과 투사성 검사(Q technique and projective tests), 임상심리학에의 적용(application to clinical psychology), 그리고 검토 및 결론(review and conclusion) 등을 논의하고 있다. 이 책의 출간은 관련 학계에 대단한 반응을 불러 일으켰다. 그리고 Q 방법론에 관한 논의를 활발하게 진행시켰다(Charlotte Banks, 1954; Cyril Burt, 1955; H. J. Eysenck, 1954; Q. McNemar, 1954; L. J. Cronbach & G. C. Glueck, 1954; R. L. Ackoff, 1955; C. P. Gerchenson, 1955; B. Glueck, 1954; R. H. Turner, 1955). The Study of Behavior 이래 Q 방법론에 관한 논의와 저서가 많이 있었으나, 이와 비교할 만한 것은 없다고 한다(B. Mckeown & D. Thomas, 1988. p. 75). 윌리엄 스티븐슨은 1961년에 세 번에 걸쳐 Psychological Record에 Q 방법론의 철학적 심리학적 기초를 논의했다. 그리고 1967

년에는 The Play Theory of Mass Communication를 발표했다. 이는 Q 방법론의 원리를 요약하고 Q 방법론을 정치, 언론, 마케팅 등의 연구에 적용하는 방법을 제시하는 것이다.

The Study of Behavior의 출간 이래 Q 방법론과 이를 적용하는 연구가 활발히 이루어졌다. 지난 30~40여 년 동안 Q 방법론은 일반원리, 생리 지각학습(학습, 기억, 사고), 행동(행동, 욕구, 의지, 감정, 정서), 발달, 특수교육, 임상(임상, 검사, 상담, 조언), 사회(사회, 집단, 문화, 산업), 직업지도 등 분야의 연구에 활용되어 왔다(齊藤耕二·淸水利信, 1958). 주로 이론검증, 특성의 유형화 연구, 심리치료 및 상담 전문의 변화연구, 심리검사의 타당화 등의 교육과 심리의 분야뿐만 아니라 정치학, 사회학, 경영학, 언론, 광고 등의 분야에도 널리 적용되어 왔다.

Q 방법론에 관련된 연구는 1996년 5월 당시, ERIC과 PSYINFO에 수록된 것을 모두 합하면 850여 편에 이른다(이건인, 1996, p.30). 이들 연구물은 그 대상과 주제 및

내용이 매우 다양하다.

[생각해 봅시다!]

---

* 여러분이 생각하는 Q와 연결할 수 있는 이슈는 무엇입니까?

* Q의 창시자와 발전공헌자를 알아봅시다.

3. Q-Methodology Analysis의
   의미와 평가

　현재까지 사회과학 분야에 있어서 과학성 제고를 위한 노력과 경향은 오랜 기간 계속되었다. 행태주의라는 학문적 풍조는 사회과학의 과학성 제고에는 기여한 바가 컸으나 사회과학이 사회가 요구하는 가치를 제공하는 데에는 실패했다는 비판이 제기되었다. 후기행태주의, 탈행태주의, 현상학의 등장은 이러한 비판을 기초로 하고 있다. 행태주의에 대한 비판과 더불어 우리의 관심을 끌었던 방법론 중의 하나가 Q 방법론이다. 1930년대에 최초로 발표되었음에도 학자들의 많은 관심을 끌지 못하다가 후기행태주의의 등장으로 새로운 방법론으로 인식되면서 활발히 논의되기 시작하였다.

한국의 경우 1970년대에 미국에서 유학한 학자들이 국내에 소개한 이후 콘텐츠방송학, 광고학, 정치행정학, 정신분석학, 간호학 분야에서 사용되고 있다. 그러나 국내에 발표된 논문들을 분석하면 Q 방법론에 대한 정확한 이해없이 사용된 예가 많다. Q 방법론은 연구 대상자의 자아참조(Self-reference)에 따라 행태와 태도를 결정하며, 변수의 선험적 의미가 주어지지 않는다. 연구 대상자의 내적 관점에 따라 행태와 태도가 결정되는 특징을 갖고 있다.

최근 Q 방법론의 효용성은 전통적 행태주의 접근방법에 대한 회의와 비판이 가속화되는 상황에서 확인되었다. 행태주의적 접근방법에 충실한 R 방법론에 의한 연구는 대부분 과학적 지식의 창출이라는 명분 하에 지식의 성격에 초점을 맞추었다. 그러나 R 방법론에 의한 지식은 2가지 측면에서 비판의 대상이 되었다. 첫째, R 방법론에 의한 사회과학적 지식은 사회 구성원 가운데 권력을 가진 계층에 적합한 지식으로 사회의 소외 계층에는 적용될 수 없다는 비판이 1960년대에 제기되었다. R 방법론에 의한 지식은 기존의 정치권력 구조를 강화하는 데에 이용된다는 것이다.

둘째의 비판은 첫째의 비판과 밀접하게 관련되어 있다. R 방법론에 기초한 지식은 사회의 현상과 상황에 적절하지 못한 잘못된 정보를 제공함으로써 정치·행정의 정책과정에 오류를 낳게 한다. 이러한 비판과 함께 정치·행정학에 있어서 Q 방법론의 활용은 실용적, 철학적 측면에서 효용성을 갖고 있다.[4] 정치·행정가들은 R 방법론이 추구하는 바와 같은 지식의 성격보다는 그들이 어떻게 그들의 업무를 수행하고 있는가하는 실용적 측면에 보다 많은 시간을 소요하고 있다. 정치·행정가들은 정책과정에 다양한 가치의 발견에 보다 관심을 갖고 있다. 이러한 상황을 감안할 때 Q 방법론이 실용적 측면에서 효용성이 있다고 할 수 있다.

---

4) Brown, S., D. During & S. Selden, 1999.

정치·행정가들의 근무환경과 특성을 감안할 때 Q 방법론의 효용성은 더욱 커진다. 정치·행정가들이 객관적 가설, 과학적 지식을 믿고 있지만 그들은 과학적 방법에 익숙하지 않을 뿐만 아니라 과학적 방법에 관심도 적은 편이다. 정치·행정가들의 문제 접근방식이 현상학적이라는 사실도 정치·행정학 분야에 있어서 Q 방법론의 효용을 높이고 있다.

실제의 정책과정을 보면 다양한 가치와 의견, 견해들이 대립되는 것이 일반적이다. 이러한 다양한 의견, 견해, 가치 등을 발견하는데 Q 방법론의 효용성이 있다. 끝으로 Q 방법론이 효율적, 경제적이라는 점도 Q 방법론의 매력이다. 적은 수의 연구 대상을 중심으로 연구가 가능하기 때문에 R 방법론에 비교하여 적은 비용과 시간이 소요된다.

정치·행정철학적 관점에서도 Q 방법론의 효용성을 확인할 수 있다. 행태주의적 접근방법에 대한 비판은 1960년대, 1970년대 신행정학의 흐름을 낳았다. 후기 행태주의로 특징되는 신행정학의 견해와 Q 방법론은 서로 양립이 가능하다. 신행정학의 견해에 따르면 정책과정이 현상학적, 이념적, 해석적이라고 보기 때문이다.

정치학적 관점에서도 후기 행태주의자들은 행태주의적 접근방법은 잘못된 지식을 낳을 뿐만 아니라, 사회의 불평등을 악화시키고 있다고 비판하였다.[5] 다양한 이익집단에 의한 자유민주주의는 특권층을 옹호하는 경향이 있기 때문에 그 대안으로 다양한 주장이 개진될 수 있는 대중적 민주주의(Discursive)를 옹호하는 관점도 Q 방법론의 효용성을 인정하고 있다. 반면, 실증주의자들은 지식의 가장 두드러진 특징을 그것의 검증가능성에 있다고 보며, 과학의 경험적 기초는 공적으로 관찰될 수 있는 사물이나 현상을 지칭하는 진술들로 이루어져 있는 것으로 파악했다. 그러나 최근 이러한 실증주의는 많은 비판에 직면해 있다. 특히 인간의 주관성을 강조하는 인문학적 전통의 학자들에 의해 많은 비판을 받고 있는 것이다.[6]

---

5) Dryzek, J., 1990.

Q 방법론의 철학은 이러한 문제로부터 출발, 논리 실증주의 방법에 대한 비판과 그 대안으로 발전되었다. 첫째, 자연현상에는 가치구조가 개입되지 않지만 사회 안에서의 인간은 특수한 의미와 적합성의 구조를 가지므로 인간의 주관성을 배제해서는 인간의 본질과 사회현상을 제대로 연구할 수 없다는 것이다. 둘째, 논리 실증주의에서 바라보는 사회적 사실은 자연현상과 마찬가지로 이미 구성된(pre-constituted) 것으로 간주하지만 사회적 현실은 의미적으로 구성되어지기(constructed) 때문에 의미의 해석을 통한 이해(understanding)의 방법이 필요한 것이라는 주장이다.

즉, Q 방법론은 '외부로부터 설명'하는 방법이 아니라 '내부로부터 이해'하는 접근방법임을 의미한다. 이는 연구자의 조작적 정의(operational definition)가 아닌 응답자 스스로 그들의 의견과 의미를 만들어 가는 operant definition의 개념을 중요하게 여긴다. 따라서 여기에 사용되는 진술문(Q-statement)은 모두 응답자의 자아참조적 의견 항목으

---

6) 김홍규, 1996, p.22.

로 구성되어있다.

물론 Stephenson은 경험주의 방법론이 갖는 한계와 오류를 극복하기 위해 이해의 방법으로 Q 방법론을 주창하고 있지만 해석학이나 현상학에서 제시하는 것처럼 다소 애매모호하고 주관적인 해석방법과는 거리를 두고 있다.[7]

다음으로, Q 방법론 관련 논의사항을 살펴보면, 1950년대까지 Q 방법론과 이를 적용하는 연구가 활발히 이루어져 왔다. 지난 50여 년 동안 Q 방법론은 일반원리, 생리 지각학습(학습, 기억, 사고), 행동(행동, 욕구, 의지, 감정, 정서), 발달, 특수교육, 임상(임상, 검사, 상담, 조언), 사회(사회, 집단, 문화, 산업), 직업지도 등 분야의 연구에 활용되어 왔다.[8] 그 이후 주로 이론검증, 특성의 유형화 연구, 심리치료 및 상담 전문의 변화연구, 심리검사의 타당화 등의 교육과 심리의 분야뿐만 아니라 정치학, 사회학, 경영학, 언론, 광고 등의 분야에도 널리 적용되어 왔다.

---

7) 김홍규, 앞의 논문.
8) 齊藤耕二·情水利信, 1959.

Q 방법론에 관련된 연구는 1996년까지 'ERIC'과 'PPSYINFO'에 수록된 것을 모두 합하면 850여 편이나 된다.[9] 이들 연구물은 그 대상과 주제 및 내용이 매우 다양하다. 이건인(1996)의 분석에 따르면 이들 연구물들은 주로 '방법론으로서의 Q 방법론의 특징, Q-SET의 개발과 그 타당성, 사람의 군집 유형, 인간관계 및 의사소통, 지도성 유형, 부모의 양육태도와 애착 유형, 학교풍토와 학교와 지역사회와의 협력 양성, 교사의 행동, 태도, 교수형태와 학생의 학업성적, 아동과 청소년의 사회성, 학습과 훈련 프로그램의 효과 및 유행, 소비자 행동과 관리 경영행동, 간호사의 행동과 간호 행동, 병의 진단, 인성 및 자아개념, 스트레스와 적응, 상담행동과 상담 효과, 기타' 등에 관한 것이라고 한다. ERIC에 수록된 Q 방법론과 관련 연구들의 분석[10]에 따르면, Q연구물이 1996년 4월까지 303편이 수록되어 있다. 이들은 1960년대의 것이 46편, 1970년대의 것이 114편, 1980년대의 것이 98편 그리고 1996년 4월까지

---

9) 이건인, 1996, p.30.
10) 백용덕·김성수, 1998, pp.44-71.

의 것이 45편이다. 이들의 내용은 1) Q-set의 개발과 타당화, 2) 유아 및 아동교육, 3) 교과교육, 4) 교육과정 개발 및 설계, 5) 교수 및 학습, 그리고 6) 직업 및 진로 교육 등에 관한 것이다.

지금까지 국내의 연구는 상당히 미흡하다고 볼 수 있다. 교육과 심리, 보건 및 의료, 언론과 소비자 등과 관련하여 다양한 분야로 연구되어 왔다. 그러나 '리서치' 중심의 연구와 달리 Q연구의 부진 이유 2가지는 Q 방법론에 관한 이해가 확산되지 못한 것과 Q 방법론의 이론과 그 적용의 어려움이라고 할 수 있을 것이다. Q 방법론은 연구대상의 특정 변인을 규정하고 그 변인을 대표하는 진술문을 수집 또는 작성하여, 그 특정 변인의 구조에 적합하다고 여겨지는 적은 대상자로 하여금 준비한 진술문을 대상자가 주관적으로 정한 기준에 따라 정상 또는 준 정상분포가 되도록 분류하고, 이를 상관분석, 변량분석, 요인분석과 요인정렬의 순서로 통계 처리한다. 변량분석과 요인분석 등의 통계적 처리 능력 없이는 Q 방법론적 연구가 제약을 받는다.

다음으로, Q 방법론의 개념적 측면을 살펴보면 다음과 같다. 윌리엄 스티븐슨[11]에 의하면, Q 방법론은 개인을 연구하기 위한 일련의 철학적, 심리학적, 통계학적, 심리측정학적 관념이라고 한다. 그리고 Q 방법론을 이행하는데 사용되는 일련의 절차를 Q기법이라고 한다.[12] 맥키온과 토마스[13]에 의하면 Q 방법론은 상관관계와 요인분석 등의 통계적 방법을 적용하여 인간의 주관성(human subjectivity)을 체계적으로 그리고 엄밀한 수량적 방법으로 연구하는 독특한 심리측정학적 조작적 원리라고 한다. 여기서 주관성은 개인적으로 또는 사회적으로 중요한 것에 대한 사적 견해(an individual point of view)를 말한다. 주관성, 곧 사적 견해는 체계적으로 그리고 정밀하고 깐깐하게 연구될 수 없는 것으로 여겨 왔는데,[14] Q 방법론의 대두가 이 같은 고정관념을 바꾸어 놓았다.

---

11) William Stephenson, 1953.
12) Kerlinger, 1986, p.507.
13) R. Mckeown & D. Thomas, 1988, p.7.
14) R. Mckeown & D. Thomas, 위의 논문.

Q 방법론은 개인의 주관성을 과학적으로 연구하는 심리측정학적 조작적 원리로서 연구하는 하나의 연구방법론이다. Q 방법론에서 말하는 주관성은 소통할 수 있는 것(communicable)이며, 항상 자기 조회(self-reference)에 의한다는 두 가지 전제에 바탕을 두고 있다. 주관적 의사소통(subjective communication)은 객관적 분석과 이해가 가능하다. 그리고 이 같은 소통을 연구하는 분석적 방법은 그 과정에서 자기 조회의 본질을 파괴하거나 변형하지 않는다. Q 방법론의 주된 관심은 자기 조회가 연구자에 의해 타협되거나 연구자에 의한 외적 조회 체제와 혼란되지 않고 잘 보존되도록 하는 것이다(R. Mckeown & D. Thomas, 앞의 논문). 개인의 주관성은 그 자신의 견해에 불과하다. 일상생활에서 흔히 말하는 "내가 관계하는 한...(as for as I'm concerned)" 또는 "내 생각으로는...(in my opinion)" 등과 같은 것이다.[15]

---

15) S. R. Brown, 1980, p.46.

종합하자면, Q 방법론의 장·단점을 감안할 때 Q 방법론으로 처리할 수 없는 부분은 R 방법론에 의하여 보완하고, R 방법론으로 해결할 수 없는 영역은 Q 방법론으로 해결할 수 있을 것이다. 따라서 Q 방법론과 R 방법론은 상호 배타적이라기보다는 상호보완적으로 사회과학의 발전에 기여할 수 있을 것이다.

이러한 논의를 중심으로 Q 방법론은 해당 전문가들의 수용행태 유형을 구조화하고 유형별 특성을 파악, 기술하고 설명하는데 좀 더 발견적이고 가설생성적이며, 수용자의 자아구조(schema) 속에 있는 요인들까지 파악할 수 있다는 장점이 있다.

 [생각해 봅시다!]

* Q에 관한 고정관념은 무엇입니까?

4. 스티븐슨과 Q이론

1) 유희이론의 적용

　매스 커뮤니케이션 이론은 1924년 출발부터 사람들의 태도, 신념 그리고 행동에 미치는 대중매체의 영향력에 집중되었다. 그러나 그 증거는 거의 발전되지 못하고 심지어 매스 커뮤니케이션 연구는 "사양길에 접어들었다"는 주장이 등장하게 되었다.

　William Stephenson은 매스미디어를 설득매체로 연구하는 것은 커다란 오류를 범하는 것으로 지적하면서 매스 커뮤니케이션이 할 수 있는 것은 기껏해야 사람들로 하여금 주관적 유희(subjective play)에 빠져들게 할 뿐이라 주장했다. 사람들은 커뮤니케이션을 대개 목적에 얽매이지 않고 재미(fun)로 이를 즐기는 특성을 갖고 있다는 것이다.

따라서 유희에 대한 고찰 없이는 매스 커뮤니케이션을 제대로 이해할 수 없으며 객관적 의미에서 사실에 관한 정보 전달에 초점을 두는 정보이론(information theory)보다는 주관적 커뮤니케이션 이론, 즉 유희이론(play theory)을 더욱 필요로 한다는 것이다.

그러나 커뮤니케이션의 유희적 접근에 대한 학술적 고찰은 그렇게 많이 이루어지지 않았다. 가설을 연역하고 검증하며 또 이론화시키는데 있어서 유희란 개념이 '과학적'이라고 생각하고 있지 않기 때문이다.

2) 주관성과 객관성의 종합

William Stephenson은 커뮤니케이션의 이러한 유희적 요소를 Q 방법론으로 해결해 나가며 이론을 발전시켰다. 그는 유희가 갖는 주관성(subjectivity)을 과학의 대상에서 제외시키는 것은 매우 위험한 것이라고 지적하면서 유희의 주관적 측면을 강조하였다. 즉 과학에 있어 주관적 측면을 강조하면서 주관성과 객관성 사이의 긴장을 해소시킬 수

있는 방안으로 Q 방법론을 제안한 것이다.16)

　사회과학에 있어 주관성과 객관성의 문제는 데카르트의 이분법적 사고 구조 속에 오랜 기간 논란의 대상이 되어 왔다. 실증성의 개념으로 객관성을 정의하려는 실증주의자들은 주로 계량적 접근방법을 이용해 세계를 설명하는데 초점을 맞춘다.

　넓은 의미의 실증주의가 표방하는 원리는 과학적 경험주의로 집약된다. 그들은 자연과학적 방법을 모든 진리 탐구를 위한 최선의 방법으로 보았고, 사회 현상의 연구에도 적용될 수 있다고 생각한다. 따라서 실증주의자들은 지식의 가장 두드러진 특징을 그것의 검증가능성에 있다고 보며, 과학의 경험적 기조는 공적으로 관찰될 수 있는 사물이나 현상을 지칭하는 진술들로 이루어져 있는 것으로 파악했다.

　그러나 최근 이러한 실증주의는 많은 비판에 직면해 있다. 특히 인간의 주관성을 강조하는 인문학적 전통의

---

16) 김홍규, "Q 방법론의 이해와 적용", 언론학논선⑦ 참조.

학자들에 의해 많은 비판을 받고 있는 것이다.[17]

Q 방법론의 철학은 이러한 문제로부터 출발, 논리 실증주의 방법에 대한 비판과 그 대안으로 발전되었다.

첫째, 자연현상에는 가치구조가 개입되지 않지만 사회 안에서의 인간은 특수한 의미와 적합성의 구조를 가지므로 인간의 주관성을 배제해서는 인간의 본질과 사회현상을 제대로 연구할 수 없다는 것이다. 둘째, 논리 실증주의에서 바라보는 사회적 사실은 자연현상과 마찬가지로 이미 구성된(pre-constituted) 것으로 간주하지만 사회적 현실은 의미적으로 구성되기(constructed) 때문에 의미의 해석을 통한 이해(understanding)의 방법이 필요한 것이라는 주장이다.

즉, Q 방법론은 '외부로부터 설명'하는 방법이 아니라 '내부로부터 이해'하는 접근방법임을 의미한다. 이는 연구자의 조작적 정의(operational definition)가 아닌 응답자 스스로 그들의 의견과 의미를 만들어 가는 operant definition의 개념을 중요하게 여긴다. 따라서 여기에 사용되는 진술

---

17) 김흥규, "주관성과 객관성의 종합", -한국주관성연구학회 제9차 학술발표회 주제문-, p.22.

문(Q-statement)은 모두 응답자의 자아 참조적 의견 항목으로 구성되어 있다.

물론 Stephenson은 경험주의 방법론이 갖는 한계와 오류를 극복하기 위해 이해의 방법으로 Q 방법론을 주창하고 있지만 해석학이나 현상학에서 제시하는 것처럼 다소 애매모호하고 주관적인 해석방법과는 거리를 두고 있다.[18]

3) 양자이론(Quantum Theory)의 적용

Stephenson은 보이지 않고 경험하지 못하는 현상, 따라서 다루기가 어렵고 논박할 수 없는 문제, 예컨대 원자 입자나 인간의 마음속에서의 내부적 활동에 대해 양자역학이 어떻게 접근할 수 있는가에 관심을 가졌다. 연구자가 직접적으로 관찰할 수 없는 아원자(subatomic) 수준에 관한 것으로 아원자의 미립자 상태는 한때 자연의 진리를 나타낸다고 생각했던 당구공 구조로 설명할 수 있는 그런 기계론적이며 인과적 발생으로는 설명할 수 없다는 것이

---

18) 김홍규, 앞의 논문.

다. 즉, 자연의 본질은 서로 상호작용 속에서 위치와 속도를 달리하는 아원자라는 것이다. 그러나 아원자의 미립자는 그것이 측정되기 전까지는 어떤 위치를 전혀 갖지 않는다. 따라서 우리가 어떤 측정도구를 갖고 전자를 발행시킬 때에 비로소 그들은 정확한 위치를 갖게 되는 것이다.[19]

양자이론 중 불확정성(complementarity)의 원리는 아원자의 발생이 상호배타적이지 않으며, 일차원적이거나 이벤트의 인과론적 연속성도 없다는 것이다. 따라서 아원자 미립자의 위치와 속도를 예측하기 위해서 과학자는 많은 가능한 해법들이 동시에 존재할 수 있다고 반드시 가정해야만 한다. 아원자 이벤트를 측정함으로써 한 이벤트가 발생할 것으로 예측할 수도 있고 또는 다른 가능성의 범위에 대해 우선적일 수도 있는 것이다. 그러나 이때 전체적인 범위는 그대로 존재하며 해석시 매우 중요하다. 한 현상의 변화, 즉 상이한 개연성 상태는 아원자 이벤트의 연구와 해석시 언제나 고려되어야 한다는 것이다. Stephenson은

---

19) G. Johnson, "*New mind, no clother*", *The Science*, 30:4, 1990, p. 48; 김홍규, 앞의 논문에서 재인용.

아원자 세계의 모호성에 대해 "어떤 상황에서 대조적인 현상이 있다면 그것에 대한 상이한 측면도 동등하게 다루어져야 함은 필수적이다"라고 강조했다.

이는 불확정성이란 개념 때문에 아원자 미립자나 인간 마음의 내적 작용을 다룰 때는 조작적 정의와 경험주의적 방법을 적용하기에 앞서 모든 개연성 상태가 스스로 존재하며 결정하는 것임을 전제해야 한다는 뜻이다. 따라서 측정과정에서 연구자는 개연성 상태의 기반을 변경하거나 뒤섞어 새로운 조합이 처음에 기대했던 것 이상으로 흥미 있는 사실을 만들어 낼 수도 있다. 그러므로 연구자가 직접 경험할 수 없는 이 세상의 모든 이벤트는 다원적(pluralistic)이며, 동시적(simultaneous)이며, 공존적(coexist)이며, 한정적(finite)이며, 총체적(collectively exhaustive)인 것이다.[20] 측정시 변화하는 것은 정확하게 고정될 수 없는 모집단 특성이 재배열되는 것이지만, 그것은 한정된 범위 내에서

---

[20] Robert Logan, "*Complementarity, pshychology and mass communication: The contributions of William Stephenson*", 1902~1989, MCR, 18: 1~2, 1991, p. 28; 김홍규, 앞의 논문에서 재인용.

이러한 환경에 우선적이라 할 수 없다.

양자이론, 특히 불확정성의 원리는 우리가 경험할 수 없는 이벤트를 연구할 때 복잡한 현상을 상호 배타적인 혹은 폐쇄된 용어로 환언시켜서는 안 된다는 것이다. 그것보다는 어떻게 사건을 재배열하는가, 즉 가능성의 범위 내에서의 변화를 발견해야 하는 것이다. 따라서 경험적 측정 도구의 역할은 새로운 가설을 탐구하고 발견하는 것이며, 다면적인 가능성의 한정된 범위 안에서 어떻게 경험이 변화하는 가를 찾아내는 것이다. 양자이론의 전제는 세상의 현상과 관찰자는 상호작용하기 때문에 개인의 현실세계에 대한 지각뿐만 아니라 현실세계 자체가 각자에게 매우 독특하다는 것이다. 이는 결국 각 개인의 독특한 자아참조의 전체틀(concourse) 속에서의 역동적 과정을 어떻게 이행하는가에 달려있다.

 [생각해 봅시다!]

* Q에 관한 철학적 관념과 개념에 대해서 논의합시다.

5. Q 방법론의 이론적 배경과 적용

1) 소개

사회과학 분야에 있어서 과학성 제고를 위한 노력과 경향은 오랜 기간 계속되었다. 행태주의라는 학문적 풍조는 사회과학의 과학성 제고에는 기여한 바가 컸으나 사회과학이 사회가 요구하는 가치를 제공하는 데에는 실패했다는 비판이 제기되었다. 후기행태주의, 탈행태주의, 현상학의 등장은 이러한 비판을 기초로 하고 있다.

행태주의에 대한 비판과 더불어 우리의 관심을 끌었던 방법론 중의 하나가 Q 방법론이다(Brown, 1980). 1930년대에 최초로 발표되었음에도 학자들의 많은 관심을 끌지 못하다가 후기 행태주의의 등장으로 새로운 방법론으로 인식되면서 활발히 논의되기 시작하였다.

우리나라의 경우 1970년대에 미국에서 유학한 학자들이 국내에 소개한 이후 신문방송학, 광고학, 정치행정학, 정신분석학, 간호학 분야에서 사용되고 있다. 그러나 국내에 발표된 논문들을 분석하면 Q 방법론에 대한 정확한 이해 없이 사용된 예가 많다. 이러한 국내적 상황이 본 논문을 집필하게 된 배경이다.

이하 내용에서는 Q 방법론의 발전적 역사, 이론적 배경, 전통적 방법론(R 방법론)과의 차이, Q 방법론의 효용성, Q 방법론에 대한 비판 등을 논의하였다.

2) Q 방법론의 발전적 역사

방법론의 새로운 개발은 새로운 지식을 탐구하기 위한 노력의 결과인 경우가 많다. 정신의 창조적 가능성을 믿었던 스페어민(Spearman)의 연구 결과인 요인분석(Factor Analysis)도 그러한 예에 속한다.

스페어만의 연구조교로서 그의 철학을 – 정신의 창조적 가능성 – 믿었던 스테펜슨(Stephenson)에 의한 창조물이 Q 방법론이다. 1935년 영국의 과학적 학술지인 Nature 의 기고에서 Q 방법론의 가능성을 시사하였다.

물리학자로서 물리학의 기초를 가졌던 스테펜슨은 심리학자로 변신하여 인간의 행동, 특히 정신의 창조적 가능성을 측정하기 위한 다양한 연구 결과 전통적인 요인분석을 Q 요인분석으로 전환할 수 있는 가능성을 시사하였다. 전통적인 요인분석은 인간의 특성들의 — 지성, 체중, 키, 학력 등 — 상관관계에 기초하여 발전된 반면 Q 요인분석은 인간들 간의 상관관계에 기초할 수 있다는 가능성을 개진하였다.

그 후 스테펜슨의 실체적인 측면에서의 학문적 노력은 신문학으로 발전되었고, 아울러 그의 방법론적 연구는 Q 방법론의 이론적 발전 및 Q 방법론의 대중적 보급에 크게 기여하였다. 특히 Q 방법론의 대중적 보급은 스테펜슨의 제자인 브라운(Brown) 교수에 의하여 이루어졌다. 스페펜슨은 1953년 그의 저서 The Study of Behavior에서 Q 방법론에 관하여 상세히 설명하였다.

1953년 스테펜슨의 저서는 심층적으로 물리학과 신문학을 토대로 작성되었기 때문에 Q 방법론의 설명에는 적합하였으나 대중적 접근에는 어려움이 있다는 비판이 제기되었다. 이러한 비판을 토대로 브라운 교수는 1980년 Political Subjectivity라는 저서를 통하여 보다 용이하게 Q 방법론의 이해와 대중적 보급에 크게 기여하였다. Q 방법론이 신문학 분야에서 정치·행정학 분야에 확대되는 계기가 되었다.

Q 방법론의 창안에서부터 현재에 이르기까지 Q 방법론에 대한 비판과 오해가 적지 않았다. Q 방법론이 전통적인 요인분석의 행렬 계산 방법에서 종렬과 횡렬을 단순히 교체한 것이라는 지적이 대표적인 오해였다. 따라서 다음 장에서는 Q 방법론의 이론적 배경에 관하여 논의하였다.

3) Q 방법론의 이론적 배경

Q 방법론의 창시자인 스테펜슨은 물리학, 심리학, 신문방송학 등의 학문적 배경을 갖고 있다. Q 방법론은 스테펜슨의 학문적 배경과 밀접하게 관련되어 있다. Q 방법론의

이론적 근거는 스테펜슨의 학문적 배경, 즉 물리학의 양자이론(Quantum Theory)과 집합이론(Concourse)에서 찾을 수 있다.

가. 양자이론(Quantum Theory)

정신의 창조성에 관심과 노력을 경주하였던 심리통계학자들은 요인분석과 양자이론의 행렬식이 수학적으로 동일하다는 것을 발견하였다. 버트(Burt)같은 전통적 심리통계학자들은 조작적 정의(Operational Definition)를 통하여 변수들의 선험적 의미에 대한 변량을 측정하였으며, 이 경우에 요인분석과 양자이론은 유사(Analogy)에 불과하다.

에너지의 이동 및 상태와 밀접한 관련이 있는 양자이론은 스테펜슨의 관심과 동일하였다. 연구 대상자에게 변수들의 조작적 정의를 통하여 작성된 선험적 의미에 대한 변량측정보다는 연구대상자의 자기참조(Self reference)에 의하여 표시하는 변량이 양자이론의 성격과 동일하다고 스테펜슨은 판단하였다.

연구대상자가 자기참조에 따라 표시하는 변량은 상호관계에 따라 결정되는 동적인 면에서 양자역학의 이론과 동일하며, 정신의 창조성을 확인하는데 효용성이 있다고 주장하였다.

정신의 창조성을 탐구하였던 학자들은 창조성의 연원을 공유(Con or Sharing)에서 찾았다. 정치·행정 등 다양한 분야에서의 논의가 생각이나 아이디어를 교환 또는 공유하는 데에서부터 출발하고 있기 때문에 생각이나 아이디어의 전달가능성(Communicability)이 정신의 창조성에 중요한 요인으로 작용하고 있다.

하나의 생각이나 아이디어가 확산되면 다른 생각이나 아이디어에 영향을 미치게 되며, 이러한 과정이 계속되어 정신의 창조성이 이루어지는 것이다. 생각의 전달가능성은 불확정적이며, 논란의 대상이 되며, 본질적으로 주관적이다(Brown et al., 1999).

아이디어의 전달가능성을 Q 방법론에서는 집합(Conurse)라고 부른다. 집합은 사회의 기초로서, 구성원과의 윤

활유 역할을 하고 있다. 집합이 사회에 존재하고 있는 문제점과 문제점 해결의 근거가 된다.

Q 방법론에서는 아이디어의 전달가능성이 — 집합(Concourse) — 기본적 요소 중의 하나가 된다. 집합을 통하여 연구 대상자간의 아이디어와 생각이 교환되며, 새로운 창조적 아이디어가 발생된다.

4) Q 방법론과 전통적 방법론과의 차이

인간의 행태나 태도를 연구하려는 행태주의적 전통은 연구자의 관점에서 변수의 조작적 정의를 통하는 과정을 거쳐 과학성을 추구하였다. 연구자가 정의한 척도와 의미에 따라 연구 대상자의 행태와 태도를 측정하였다.

따라서 변수의 조작적 정의와 척도는 연구자가 정의한 바에 따라 결정되며, 연구 대상자는 연구자가 결정한 정의에 따라 행태와 태도를 결정한다. 연구는 연구자 외적 관점에서 이루어진다.

반면 Q 방법론은 연구 대상자의 자아참조(Selfeference)

에 따라 행태와 태도를 결정하며, 변수의 선험적 의미가 주어지지 않는다. 연구 대상자의 내적 관점에 따라 행태와 태도가 결정되는 특징을 갖고 있다. 이러한 전통적 방법론(R 방법론)과 Q 방법론의 차이를 상론하면 다음과 같다.

첫째, 전통적 연구방법인 R 방법론은 연구 대상의 배경적 특색, 예를 들면 지성, 종교, 학력, 체중, 신장, 나이, 성별 등간의 구조적 특색을 발견하는데 사용된다. 이를 위하여 연구자는 지성, 종교 등에 관한 조작적 정의와 변수의 척도를 개발하고, 연구 대상자는 연구자의 조작적 정의에 따라 연구 대상자의 배경적 특색을 나타낸다.

반면 Q 방법론은 연구 대상자의 특정 주제 및 자극에 대한 의견이나 태도의 구조를 확인하는데 사용된다. R 방법론에 있어서와 같이 연구자가 사전에 변수에 대한 조작적 정의와 척도를 결정하지 않고 연구자가 작성한 집합(Concourse)를 통한 연구 대상자의 자아참조에 따라 연구 대상자가 자율적으로 특정한 주제나 자극에 대한 연구 대상자의 의견을 표시한다. 따라서 Q 방법론은 연구

대상자의 주관적 구조, 즉 특정 주제에 대한 유사한 견해를 가진 집단을 추출하게 된다.

따라서 전자는 연구자가 결정한 조작적 정의가 연구 대상자의 행태나 태도를 결정하고 제약한다. 반면 후자는 연구 대상자가 자율적으로 결정하기 때문에 연구자의 조작에 좌우되지 않는다.

둘째, Q 방법론의 연구 대상은 거짓과 진실에 관한 것이 아니고, 주관적 견해 즉 좋고 나쁨, 선하고 악함 등의 주관적 성격을 띠고 있다. R 방법론이 행태주의적 전통에 의하여 발전된 반면, Q 방법론은 후기 행태주의, 현상학의 발전과 맥을 같이하고 있다.

셋째, 전통적 R 방법론은 다수의 무작위 표본을 대상으로 연구 대상의 배경적 특색을 유형화하는 포괄적인 연구에 사용된다. 반면 Q 방법론은 소수의 대상, 때로는 1인의 대상에 대한 심층적인 연구에 사용된다. 이러한 특색에 감안하여 Q 방법론을 이용한 연구에 있어서는 연구 대상의 선택에 각별히 신중해야 한다. 연구 주제와 관련하여 대표적인 사람들이 참여되도록 설계하는 것이 바람직하다.

5) Q 방법론의 효용과 실용성

최근 Q 방법론의 효용성은 전통적 행태주의 접근방법에 대한 회의와 비판이 가속화되는 상황에서 확인되었다. 행태주의적 접근방법에 충실한 R 방법론에 의한 연구는 대부분 과학적 지식의 창출이라는 명분하에 지식의 성격에 초점을 맞추었다. 그러나 R 방법론에 의한 지식은 2가지 측면에서 비판의 대상이 되었다.

첫째, R 방법론에 의한 사회과학적 지식은 사회 구성원 가운데 권력을 가진 계층에 적합한 지식으로 사회의 소외 계층에는 적용될 수 없다는 비판이 1960년대에 제기되었다. R 방법론에 의한 지식은 기존의 정치권력 구조를 강화하는 데에 이용된다는 것이다.

둘째의 비판은 첫째의 비판과 밀접하게 관련되어 있다. R 방법론에 기초한 지식은 사회의 현상과 상황에 적절하지 못한 잘못된 정보를 제공함으로써 정치·행정의 정책과정에 오류를 낳게 한다.

이러한 비판과 함께 정치·행정학에 있어서 Q 방법론의 활용은 실용적, 철학적 측면에서 효용성을 갖고 있다 (Brown et al., 1999). 정치·행정가들은 R 방법론이 추구하는 바와 같은 지식의 성격보다는 그들이 어떻게 그들의 업무를 수행하고 있는가하는 실용적 측면에 보다 많은 시간을 소요하고 있다. 정치·행정가들은 정책과정에 다양한 가치의 발견에 보다 관심을 갖고 있다. 이러한 상황을 감안할 때 Q 방법론이 실용적 측면에서 효용성이 있다고 할 수 있다.

정치·행정가들의 근무환경과 특성을 감안할 때 Q 방법론의 효용성은 더욱 커진다. 정치·행정가들이 객관적 가설, 과학적 지식을 믿고 있지만 그들은 과학적 방법에 익숙하지 않을 뿐만 아니라 과학적 방법에 관심도 적은 편이다. 정치·행정가들의 문제 접근방식이 현상학적이라는 사실도 정치·행정학 분야에 있어서 Q 방법론의 효용을 높이고 있다.

실제의 정책과정을 보면 다양한 가치와 의견, 견해들이 대립되는 것이 일반적이다. 이러한 다양한 의견, 견해, 가치 등을 발견하는데 Q 방법론의 효용성이 있다. 끝으로 Q 방법론이 효율적, 경제적이라는 점도 Q 방법론의 매력이다. 적은 수의 연구 대상을 중심으로 연구가 가능하기 때문에 R 방법론에 비교하여 적은 비용과 시간이 소요된다.

 정치·행정철학적 관점에서도 Q 방법론의 효용성을 확인할 수 있다. 행태주의적 접근방법에 대한 비판은 1960년대, 1970년대 신행정학의 흐름을 낳았다. 후기 행태주의로 특징되는 신행정학의 견해와 Q 방법론은 서로 양립이 가능하다. 신행정학의 견해에 따르면 정책과정이 현상학적, 이념적, 해석적이라고 보기 때문이다.

 정치학적 관점에서도 후기 행태주의자들은 행태주의적 접근방법은 잘못된 지식을 낳을 뿐만 아니라, 사회의 불평등을 악화시키고 있다고 비판하였다(Dryzek, 1990). 다양한 이익집단에 의한 자유민주주의는 특권층을 옹호하는 경향이 있기 때문에 그 대안으로 다양한 주장이 개진될 수 있는 대중적 민주주의(Discursive)를 옹호하는 관점도 Q 방법론의 효용성을 인정하고 있다.

다음 장에서는 Q 방법론에 대한 인식분석을 실시하였다. Q 방법론의 적용과 Q 방법론에 비판이라는 차원에서 Q 방법론에 대한 인식분석을 중심으로 Q 방법론에 필요한 절차와 내용을 논의하였다.

6) Q 방법론에 대한 인식분석

가. Q 방법론의 절차

Q 방법론을 활용함에 있어서 최초의 절차는 연구주제와 관련하여 Q 진술문을 작성하는 작업이다. 그 작업이 끝나면 연구 대상자를 결정하고, 연구 대상자로부터 Q 분류 자료를 얻는 절차를 거친다. Q분류 자료를 얻게 되면 요인분석의 단계를 거쳐 분석자료를 해석하게 된다. 이러한 절차와 관련된 이슈를 논의하면 다음과 같다.

(1) Q 진술문(Q Statements)의 작성

Q 방법론을 사용한 연구의 가장 중요한 부분이 Q 진술문을 작성하는 작업이다. 연구 주제에 관한 Q 진술문은 전통적인 R 방법론에 있어서 무작위 추출한 표본의 중요성과 유사하다. Q 연구에 있어서는 연구 대상자가 변수가 되며 진술문을 분류한 연구대상의 집단이 Q 요인이 되며, 각각의 Q 요인은 작성된 진술문에 의하여 해석되기 때문이다.

 Q 진술문 작성은 연구설계의 방법에 따라 구조적, 비구조적 표본으로 구분되며, 진술문의 출처에 따라 구술형, 추출형으로 구분된다. 구술형은 연구대상자와의 면접에 따라 진술문을 작성하는 것이며, 추출형은 기존의 문헌이나 신문기사 등에서 추출한 것을 의미한다.

 Q 진술문의 중요한 구분은 구조적, 비구조적 표본의 여부이다. Q 방법론을 이용한 연구도 귀납적, 연역적인 논리의 적용이 가능한데 이러한 적용은 진술문의 작성 방법에 따라 결정된다. 비구조적 방법은 특별한 연구설계가 없고 연구 주제와 관련된 문장을 종합하는 것이다. 이론적으로 연구주제와 관련된 모든 문장이 Q 진술문이 될

수 있다. 수많은 진술문을 작성한 후 대표적 진술문을 선택하는 방법이 좋다(Kerlinger, 1973).

반면 구조적 방법에 따른 Q 진술문은 피셔식 실험 및 분산분석 설계원리(Fisherian Experimental and Analysis of Variance Design Principle)에 따라 작성된 것을 의미한다. 구조적 방법으로 진술문을 작성하는 것은 이론을 구축하는 것이다. 개인들의 특성을 측정하는 도구를 구축하는 대신에 연구대상자들을 통하여 기존의 이론을 형체화하게 된다.

(2) 통계학적 분석

연구대상자로부터 Q 자료가 구득하면 자료를 입력하여 분석단계에 들어간다. P 표본간의 상관관계를 토대로 요인분석이 이루어진다. Q 방법론에 인식분석에 관한 연구는 크게 3가지 요인으로 분류되었다. 외견상으로는 2개의 요인으로 보이지만 요인 B가 양극요인(Bipolar Factor)으로 나타났기 때문에 3개 요인으로 해석하였다(MeKeown and Thomas, 1988).

(3) Q 요인(factor)의 해석

Q 연구에 있어서 중요한 부분 중의 하나가 Q 요인의 해석이다. 연구의 결과 산출된 Q 요인은 특정 주제에 관하여 유사하게 판단 또는 생각하는 사람들의 집단이다(Brown, 1980; 김순은, 1993, 1997). 유사한 생각을 가진 집단을 나타내는 Q 요인의 해석은 주로 해당 요인의 진술문 중 극단값, 즉 +4, +3, -4, -3을 가진 진술문 등으로 해석한다.

본 연구에서 나타난 3개의 요인을 해석하면 다음과 같다.

A. Q 방법론에 대한 신중적 긍정론적 시각

Q 방법론의 정당성이나 효용성에 대해서는 스테펜슨이 Q 방법론의 개발하였던 시점부터 찬·반양론 존재하고 있다. 이에 대해서는 다음 장에서 심층적으로 논의하겠으나 본 연구의 결과도 이를 경험적으로 입증하고 있다.

무엇보다도 첫 번째 요인은 Q 방법론의 유용성을 인식하는 연구 대상자의 집단이다.

B. Q 방법론에 대한 부정적 견해

부정 요인의 특징은 그 동안 Q 방법론에 관하여 제기된 논의 중 긍정적 주장을 나타내는 진술문에는 양의 높은 점수를, 부정적 주장을 표시하는 진술문에서 부의 높은 점수를 부여함으로써 Q 방법론에 대하여 부정적 견해를 강력하게 표시하고 있는 것으로 나타났다.

7) Q 방법론에 대한 비판적 분석

상기의 Q 방법론과 관련된 논쟁은 50년 이상 끊임없이 계속되었다. 일반적으로 논쟁의 대상이 되었던 부분은 앞 장의 인식분석에서도 적절히 입증되었다. 무엇보다도 Q 방법론의 효용성에 비판적이었던 주장을 크게 요약하면 통계학적 관점에서 Q 연구 결과의 일반화, Q 분류의 방법, 통계학적 분석방법 등으로 요약할 수 있다. 이를 상론하면 다음과 같다.

가. Q 연구 결과의 일반화

Q 방법론에 대하여 가장 비판적인 부분은 연구 대상자의 추출방법과 규모와 관련되어 있다. 전통적인 R 방법론에서는 다수의 표본을 무작위로 추출할 것이 요구된다. 반면 Q 방법론에서는 20~0명의 적은 규모, 심지어는 1인의 연구 대상자를 상대로 연구를 수행할 수 있다는 것은 앞에서 논의하였다.

무작위 추출에 의하지 않고, 적은 수의 연구대상자를 토대로 산출된 Q 연구의 결과는 일반화할 수 없다는 것이 일반적 비판이었다. Q 방법론을 "가설발견의 논리"라고 명명하는 것도 Q 방법론의 이러한 특징에 기인하고 있다. 따라서 Q 연구의 결과를 일반화하기 위해서는 무작위 추출에 의한 다수의 표본에 적용하여야 한다(Kerlinger, 1973).

이러한 비판에 대하여 연구 대상자의 규모는 연구의 목적과 밀접하게 관련되어 있음에 주목할 필요가 있다. 연구의 목적을 달성하기 위하여 다수의 연구 대상자가 필요한 연구의 경우는 경제적인 측면과 물리적인 측면에서 무작위 추출에 의한 표본을 선택하여야 한다.

그러나 연구의 목적이 소수의 대상자를 하는 경우에는 일반화의 문제는 처음부터 발생하지 않는다. 예를 들면, 특정 조직 내의 문제점을 연구하는 경우에는 모집단의 규모가 특정 조직 내의 구성원에 한정하기 때문에 조직 외의 대상자를 연구의 범위에 포함시킬 필요가 발생하지 않는다.

연구의 결과가 일반화되기 위해서는 2가지 요건을 충족하여야 한다(Brown and Ungs, 1970). 하나는 자료를 제공하여야 하는 연구 대상자의 대표성이며, 또 하나는 연구의 결과가 적용될 수 있는 상황의 대표성을 의미한다. Q 방법론에 대한 비판은 주로 전자에 기인한다.

Q 방법론은 전통적인 R 방법론에 비하여 후자의 대표성이 매우 높다(Brown et al., 1999). 다양한 Q 진술문을 통하여 연구대상자는 다양한 상황을 직면하기 때문에 R 방법론이 결여하고 있는 상황의 대표성이 높다. 특히 상황적 변이가 사람에 따른 변이보다 중요하다는 점을 감안할

때 Q 방법론의 대표성은 매우 높다고 할 수 있다.

아울러 Q 방법론에 의한 연구 결과인 Q 요인들은 비슷한 견해, 관점, 가치를 가진 사람들의 집단이므로 그러한 집단의 일반적 견해이다. 비록 적은 수의 연구대상자라 하더라도 그러한 집단의 대표적 견해라고 할 수 있다.

나. Q 분류의 방법

앞장에서 논의한 바와 같이 Q 진술문은 연구자의 지시에 따라 연구 대상자가 분류한다. 그러나 연구자의 지시는 일반적으로 Q 진술문의 분류가 정규분포의 형태를 이루도록 강제 배분하는 것이 권장되고 있다 (〈표 6-3〉 참조). 이러한 분류방법에 대하여 다양한 비판이 제기되고 있다.

비판의 주장을 정리하면 다음과 같다. 우선 연구대상자가 30개 이상이 되는 Q 진술문을 연구자의 지시에 따라 분류할 인식능력을 갖추고 있지 않다. 아울러 전통적인 R 방법론에서는 질문 간에 독립성이 중요한데 Q 연구에서는 진술문 상호간에 영향력이 매우 크게 작용하고 있다.

정규분포의 형태를 띠기 위해서는 극단값을 갖는 진술문의 수가 극히 적다.

이러한 비판에 대하여 Q 방법론자의 방어는 다음과 같다. Q 연구에 있어서는 진술문의 값의 차이가 연구 대상자의 내면적인 서열적 의미만을 갖고 있기 때문에 절대적 의미의 차이를 분석하는 R 방법론과는 상이하다. 연구의 상황적 변이를 중시하는 Q 연구에 있어서는 Q 진술문간의 상호작용이 중시된다. 오류의 법칙(Law of Error)에 따르면 의미를 갖는 적은 수의 진술문이 의미가 없는 또는 의미가 적은 많은 수의 진술문보다 중요하다. 따라서 극단값을 갖는 적은 수의 진술문의 선택은 연구의 편의만을 위한 것이기 때문에 통계학적인 가정에 위배되지 않는다(Brown, 1999).

다. 통계학적 분석방법

연구대상자간에 상관관계가 분석되면 이를 토대로 요인분석의 단계로 발전한다. 요인이 추출되면 요인 간에 로테이션이 이루어진다. 로테이션 방법은 객관적인 방법으로 배리맥스(Varimax), 쿼타맥스(Quartimax), 이퀴맥스(Equimax) 등의 방법이 있고 주관적인 방법으로 센트로이드(Centroid) 방식이 있다.

전자 중에서는 배리맥스 방법이 자주 활용되고 있다. 배리맥스는 추출된 요인 속에 가능한 한 다수의 Q 분류(연구 대상자)를 포함시키는 방식이다. Q 연구에 있어서도 이 방식이 자주 이용되고 있다.

그러나 스티븐슨이나 브라운 교수는 주관적이고 판단적인 센트로이드 방식을 권장하고 있다. 이러한 권장에 대하여 연구의 비결정성(In-determinancy)만을 높인다는 비판이 제기되고 있다.

상황적 변이가 강조되는 Q 연구에 있어서는 특정 연구대상자에 초점을 맞출 수 있는 센트로이드 방식이 상황적 적실성을 높이는 데 효용이 높다. 이러한 주장에 근거할 때 아이겐 값이 1미만인 경우의 요인도 의미있는 요인으로 해석할 수 있다. Q 연구에 있어서 요인추출은 통계학적 근거뿐만 아니라 상황적 근거에 의하여 추출하는 것도 이러한 근거에 기초하고 있기 때문이다(Brown, 1980; McKeown and Thomas, 1988).

8) Q 방법론의 기여와 발전

상기에서 Q 방법론에 대한 이론적 배경과 Q 방법론에 대한 인식을 구체적인 사례를 통하여 분석하였다. 사례분석은 기존의 Q 방법론에 대한 이론적 논쟁을 경험적으로 입증하고 있다.

Q 방법론을 둘러싼 이론적 논쟁을 물론 구체적인 사례분석에서 보았듯이 Q 방법론은 장점과 단점을 함께 지니고 있다. 적은 수의 연구대상자를 상대로 연구가 진행되기 때문에 연구 대상자의 배경적 변수와 Q 요인 간의 관계를 일반화하는 데에는 이론이 있을 수 있다.

그럼에도 불구하고 Q 방법론은 주관성을 과학적으로 측정하는데 효용이 있다. 인간의 주관성은 입증하기 쉽지 않지만, 주관성은 일정한 구조와 형태를 띠고 있다. 연구를 위하여 주관성의 구조와 형태를 측정하는 데에 Q 방법론의 효용성이 있다(Brown, 1980).

"Q 방법론은 주관성의 과학화에 기초를 제공한 일종의 철학적, 심리적, 통계적, 그리고 계량심리적 도구이다. Q 방법론의 우수한 장점은 인간행위의 주관적인 면 —인간의 주관성— 관찰과 측정에 있다. 주관성이라 함은 동적인 상황 속에서 자결적(Operantly)으로 정의되는 개인의 관점 및 관념을 말한다"(김순은, 1997, p.6). 정치, 행정분야에 있어서 정책과정에 참여하는 참가자들의 주관성이 정책결과에 미치는 영향이 매우 큰 점을 감안하면 주관성을 과학적으로 측정할 수 있는 Q 방법론의 효용성이 크다고 할 수 있다.

종합하면, Q 방법론의 장·단점을 감안할 때 Q 방법론으로 처리할 수 없는 부분은 R 방법론에 의하여 보완하고, R 방법론으로 해결할 수 없는 영역은 Q 방법론으로 해결할 수 있을 것이다. 따라서 Q 방법론과 R 방법론은 상호 배타적이라기보다는 상호보완적으로 사회과학의 발전에 기여할 수 있을 것이다.

[생각해 봅시다!]

* Q와 R의 통계방법의 해석과 그 차이점을 논의합시다.

6. Q 방법론의 역사와 원리
: 심리학과 사회과학

　　Q 방법론은 영국의 물리학자이자 심리학자인 William Stephenson에 의해 처음 도입되었다. 그러나 Q 방법론은 영국이 아닌 미국에서 주로 적용 및 발전되어 왔는데, 심리학의 범위를 넘어 커뮤니케이션과 정치학 분야에서 가장 주목을 받아왔으며 최근에는 건강과학 분야에서도 적용되고 있다. Q 방법론의 원리는 재정립되었고, 1930년대 영국 심리학에 널리 퍼져있던 초창기의 이해 및 당시의 실질적인 적용과 함께 몇몇 차이점들이 도출되었다. 그 결론은 다음과 같나: 심리측정학적인 평가에 대한 관심과 더불어 시대에 떨어지는 뉴턴주의로의 집착은, 영국 심리학이 R 방법론을 채택하게 하고 양자론과 주관성 과학을 위해 함께 병행돼야 할 Q 방법론을 놓치는 결과를 낳았다. 그리

고 후기 근대파의 발달이 새로운 세대의 영국 심리학자들을 포함한 사회과학자들이 Q 방법론과의 관계를 재정립하는 것을 가능케 하였고, 인간행동을 이해하는데 있어서 Q 방법론이 제공하는 힘을 이용하는 것 또한 가능케 하였다.

Q 방법론은 William Stephenson(1935a)이 Nature지에 보낸 편지로 인해 소개됨으로써 나오게 되었다. Stephenson은 1926년 Durham 대학에서 박사학위를 취득한 물리학자이며, 1929년 London 대학에서 박사학위를 취득한 심리학자이다. 그는 사실연구의 발명자인 Charles Spearman의 마지막 조교로서 일했다. Spearman은 한때 그의 부하(protege)가 심리학에서 가장 창조적인 학자라고 평가했다. 그러나, 사실상 이때부터 방법론으로서의 Q의 광범위한 고찰이 논쟁의 여지가 있는 것으로 운명 지어졌으며 대부분의 학구적인 심리학에 의해 멀리하게 되었다. 오늘날 Q 방법론은 사회과학에서 널리 받아들여지고 있으나, 대부분의 경우 Q 분류(sorting)의 기술적 과정을 (미국에

서) 얻기 위해 심리학 자체에서 약간 기억되고 있다. 단지 최근에 젊은 세대의 심리학자들이 Q 방법론을 다시 연구하고 있으며, Stephenson이 50년 이상 조성해 온 시각과 함께 알려지고 있다. Stephenson의 가장 뛰어난 업적은 "행동연구:Q 기술과 그의 방법론(The Study of Behavior :Q-technique and Its Methodology, 1953)"의 저술이다. Q와 그 창시자 주변 논쟁의 몇몇은 이 출판을 반기는 여러 평론을 다시 봄으로써 알아볼 수 있다. 영국의 Charlotte banks(1954)는 즉시 "Stephenson의 원기왕성한 호전성", 그의 "생동적이며 재미있는 스타일", 그리고 그의 "새롭고 독창적인 생각" 또한 그의 혁신의 몇몇을 암시하고 있다. 이 혁신은 특히 Stern과 Burt에 의해 앞서갔던 것이다. Banks는 아마도 Burt(1955)에 의한 이 관점에 고무되었는지 모른다. Burt는 또한 Stern의 앞서의 연구를 그 자신의 입지, 말하자면 Stephenson의 반대(contra)라고 주장하려는 한 방편으로서 생각했다. "만약 우리가 어떤 상황에 있게 된 우리 자신을 측정하려고 제한한다면 아마도 사람들을 나누고 특성을 연관 짓거나, 특성을 나누고 사람을 연관지을 지도 모른다." 그래서, Burt는 항상 단지 하나로 된 자료의 행렬만이 논쟁이 되며, 나누려는 여러 방법은 그 행렬을 가로지르게(across) 된다. 가장 신랄한 비판은 아마도 Eysenck(1954)로부터 나왔다. Eysenck는 Stephenson이 그가 지금 뜻하는 바가 그가 줄곧 뜻했던 것처럼 보이는 동안, "무엇인가 오랫동안 Q 방법이라는 의미를 바꾸기 위해 솔직하지 않은 경향이 있다"며 비난했다.

미국에서 McNemar(1954)는 행동연구의 저자를 비판하기를, 그는 애매하며 "마치 Godfrey Thomson과 Cyril Burt 같은 이성을 지녔다"고 공격했으며, 특히 한 사례연구의 가치에 대해 회의적이었다. Stephenson(1954a)에게 대답하도록 만들었던 가장 완전한 비평은 다음과 같다. Cronbach와 Gleser(1954)가 카드 분류(card sorting)와 Fisher의 실험에 관한 디자인의 중요한 결합같은 기술적인 혁신을 요약했던 비평이다. 그러나 그 후 권고(warning)가 제기되었다. : "이것은 Stephenson이 학생들에게 제시했던 디자인을 모방하는 것으로부터 학생들의 개성과 사회 심리학을 실망시키는 것은 부득이하다는 것이다." 또한 Stephenson이 주장한 화려함과 부주의는 언급되었다. 결국 Turner(1955)는 Q 방법론의 창시자를 비난하기를, "잘못 위치한 논쟁거리", "사회나 현실문제와 관계가 없는 것에 대한 강조"의 "반복성", "터무니없는 주장" 만들기, 그리고 "다른 사람들이 했던 많은 일과의 뚜렷한 어색함" 이라고 했다. 그러나 또한 Q가 "의심할 여지없이 기술에 있어 두 가지 가장 중요한 최근의 기여중의 하나로 Guttman 저울과 더불어 우뚝 선다"고 결론지었다.

한때 이 방법이 학구적인 심리학과 정신측정(학) 외부에 의해 취해졌음에도 불구하고 분위기는 무엇인가 바뀌게 된다. 정신병 의학자 Bernard Glueck(1954)는 Q가 "독창성의 보편성"을 겨냥한 "오래 기다려온 기수이며 지시를 신뢰할 수 있는 구조"를 제공한다며 반겼다. OR(과학적 조사연구)의 창시자 중의 한 명인 Russell Ackoff(1955)는 "이 책은 오랫동안 심리학적인 방법론으로서 자리잡게 될 것"이라고 예견했다. 그리고 Stephenson의 "화려하고 차라리 과대 망상적인 글 솜씨"가 평가받지 못하는 동안(while nothing)에 정신요법치료사인 Lyman Wyne은 또한 그 책이 정신의학 연구자와 이와 관련된 분야에 "다양하고 즉각적인 반응"이 있을 것이라고 밝혔다. 한편, 사회 사업가인 Gershenson(1955)은 행동연구가 "저자와 비판자들 사이의 논쟁"을 조성했다고 비난하면서도, 그를 이해할 수 없게 했던 많은 것들이 그의 분야의 통계적 궤변의 부족을 막았다고 인정했다.

다음으로, Q-R 논쟁의 뿌리(The Roots of the Q-R Controversy) 측면에서 짚어보면 다음과 같다. 사실 분석적인 단계로서 Q와 R 사이 관계에 대한 많은 혼란은 다음과 같은 사실 때문에 발생했다. Cyril Burt가 의미했던 "상호 연관된 사람들"(Burt, 1937, 1940)과 Stephenson이 의미했던 것(Stephenson, 1935b, 1953), 즉 최소한 두 가지 점에서 분명히 세분되는 것들, 한 관점에 대해 동의 또는 반대에 대한 문제였다(Burt & Stephenson, 1939) :

Burt는 양쪽의 사실 체계가 하나 그리고 오직 하나인 (one and only one) 기본 자료 행렬(data matrix)에 기초하고 있다. 그 행렬은 특히 객관적인 실험(objective tests)에서 나온 점수로 채워진 것으로, 예를 들어 지식, 읽는 속도, 또는 수학적 능력 등이 있다. Stephenson에게는 두 개의 나누어지는(two separate) 자료 행렬에 주목하고 있으며, 하나는 객관적인 측정(R)을 담고 있으며, 다른 하나는 주관적인 (subjective) 종류(Q)를 내포한 자료다. Burt가 Q와 R의 상호관계를 주장했고 그래서 그가 끝까지 주장했던 원리(Burt, 1972)는 같은 전치행렬의 두 개의 행렬 조작(하나는 항, 다른 하나는 열에 의한)을 의미한다. 그런데, Stephenson(1953)은 "R과 Q 적용 양쪽에 적용되는 하나의 행렬 점수는 결코 없다"고 했다(p. 15).

초기의 발표로부터 Stephenson(1935a)는 R 방법론이 "각각을 m 실험으로 측정된(수동형으로서의 측정된) n 개인들의 표본 집단"을 의미한다고 명확히 했다. Q 방법론이

"n 다른 실험(또는 에세이, 그림, 특성 또는 다른 측정 가능한 재료)의 집단, 즉 각각이 측정되거나 m 개인에 의해 측정할 수 있는(능동형인 재다) 것이라고 밝혔다. 그전의 연구에서 혈압을 재거나 키를 잴 때 사람에게 행했다. 이것이 객관적인(objective) 방법이며 측정과 관련해서 사람의 태도는 수동적이다. 최근의 실험에서 사람은 능동적으로 무엇인가를 한다. 예를 들어, 측정할 수 있는 도구로 집단을 측정 또는 계산한다. 측정이 사람의 견지로부터 나오는 한 이것은 주관적인(subjective) 방법이다. Stephenson(1935b)이 후에 지적한 "앞서 개인들은 점수를 얻었다; 지금은 개인의 작용 때문에 실험이 점수를 대신한다(p. 19). 그리고 그가 보여준 첫 번째 실시된 실험에서 한 집단의 사람들이 즐거움의 견지에서 색깔로 구분을 짓는다는 것은 분명 주관적이다. 이러한 두 가지 방법은 어울리지 않으며(Brown, 1972) 이러한 관점에서 비상호적이며, 또한 Q 방법론이 주관성의 과학에 기초를 제공한다는 사실이다(Brown, 1944-1995).

무엇이 근본적으로 문제인가는 Stephenson(1936a)에 의해 기본적으로 제안되었고 가장 분명하게 인간을 25의 측정연구에서 보여주고 있다. - 팔 길이, 넓적다리 넓이, 발길이 둥 - 20명에 대한 각각의 측정이다(세부적인 것은 Brown 참조, 1972, 1980, p. 13). R 요인 분석을 적용했을 때 결과는 전체 신체 부위를 8개의 요소로 분할하는 것이다. 즉 어깨 넓이, 팔 길이, 손바닥 넓이, 그리고 발 길이(다른 것들 중에서)가 어떤 한 사실에서 중요하고, 가슴과 허리 넓이가 다른 사실에서 중요하다 등이다. 전체를 나누어서 부분으로 해석하는 것이 R 요인 분석이다. 그러나, 원래 자료 행렬이 바뀌었을 때(교차) 그리고 다시 분해했을 때 결과는 전체 변화의 99%를 단순한 치수로 계산하는 것이다. 그리고 인간은 신체적으로 동일하다는 사실의 반영이기도 하다. 그들의 상호관계에서 부분을 함께 유지하는 것이 Q 요소 분석이 하는 일이다.

앞서의 결과들은 같은 자료 행렬과 치수는 객관적인 방식에 의존하고 있다: 한 사람의 팔이 꽤 길고, 그 사실에 대해서 할 수 있는 것은 매우 작으며, 이것은 특성이나 인간의 관련여

부와 상관없이 사실이라는 것이다. 이것이 Burt가 본 사람의 연관성에 대한 관점이다. 그러나, Stephenson의 관점은 주관적인 자료의 개별 행렬에 연관되며, 같은 신체 부위를 "나에게 중요한" 관점에서 평가하기 위해 같은 20명 개인에게 지시한 경우에 영향을 받았다. Q 요인의 4가지 결과가 밝혀졌다. 신체 부위와 관련된 다른 두드러진 특징들이 예시에 포함되었다: 예를 들어, 첫 번째 요인은 높은 점수를 받은 눈, 머리, 입을 매우 강조했다; 두 번째 요소는 몸통, 엉덩이, 그리고 가슴이 두었다.

R 요인 분석의 결과가 같은 방식하에서의 예술적인 형식이 주어지지 않는다는 것은 주목할 만하다. 그것은 R이 현실을 간과해서 모든 훌륭한(King's)의 예술가들이 그것을 함께 되돌릴 수 없다는 사실 때문이다. Stephenson의 그것과 비교해서 사람과 연관된 Burt의 접근인 공정성의 암시를 고려한다기보다는, 오직 둘 중의 하나만이 실제의 물질인 두 현상의 실제적인 형태에서의 표현으로부터 나타난다. 팔 길이 같은 신체의 확대는 실제적인 관점으로 쉽게

그려지지만 주관성은 이 신체적인 의미에서 존재하지 않는다. 그리고 Q 방법론과 더불어 심리학 난제의 많은 부분은 이 개념의 구별에 원인이 있다. Stephenson은 물리학자로서 잘 알게 되었던 같은 과학의 종주권 하에서 주관성의 어려움을 제기하기 위해 참여하게 된다. 그리고 결국 요인 분석의 기술을 사용하게 된다. 그동안 심리학은 Spearman의 g와 Eysenck의 내향성-외향성 같은 객관적인 능력들과 일반 개념만을 생각하고 있었다. 이러한 능력과 개념은 또한 요인 같은 것도 표현되지만 주관성을 위해서는 여지가 없다(실수차이 같은 것은 제외).

Burt의 사람과 관련된 설명은 익숙한 정신 분석 세계를 계속 실행하는데 부가적인 이점이 있다: 객관적인 측정들은 연관된 특성 또한 사람을 상호 연결짓기 위한 기초라는 토대를 제공했다. 그래서 새로운 개념들은 필요하지 않으며, 단지 다른 방법으로 그들을 바라보는 것이다. Stephenson이 알고 있으나, 다른 방식으로 생각을 요구한 주관성에 대한 연구는 뉴턴의 범위와 인과관계에 있어서의 뿌리와 더불어 종래의 요인분석에서는 떠나게 되었다. 그래서 과학에서 새로운 발전방향에서 그리고 인간행동을 이해하는 선택 방법들만이 현재 인기를 얻기 시작하고 있다. 그 결과 Burt와 Stephenson 간의 중요한 차이점은 요인 분석의 역학으로 향하지 않고, 측정 가능함이 어떻게 무엇에 의해 좌우된다는 것이다.

 [생각해 봅시다!]

* Q분석과 심리학과의 관계에 대해서 논의합시다.

7. 주관성과 커뮤니케이션

　William Stephenson은 소비행위가 주관적 복합체로서 조직되는 경향을 설명하고 있는데(Stephenson, 1969) 이것은 일관적이며 특징적으로 구성된다는 것이다. 이러한 맥락에서 소비자의 스키마타를 이해하는 것은 소비행위를 파악하는데 필수적이며, 근본적인 것이다. 이제까지의 연구는 대개 소비자 혹은 목표시장을 이해하기 위해 거의 반사적으로 연령, 수입, 성별, 결혼여부, 사회계층 등 소위 인구학적 속성(demographics)을 이용해 왔다. 이러한 정보는 객관적이며, 일반적인 면에서는 어떤 종류의 소비자를 다루고 있는지를 명료화시켜 줄 수 있기 때문에 광고나 시장조사 등에서 중요시 되어왔던 것이다. 그러나 이러한 정보는 사람들이 왜 그러한 구매를 하는가에 관해 거의 알려주지 못하며, 나아가 광고 등 마케팅 활동을 위한 아이디어의 도출을 기대할 수 없게 한다.(Kim, 1996)

이러한 문제점을 해결하기 위하여 본 연구는 Q 방법론을 이용하여 소비자들의 내재된 심리구조를 파악하고 그를 통해 담배시장의 세분화를 이루는데 그 목적이 있다.

객관적으로 고찰하면 소비자의 상황, 쇼핑 시설, 광고의 상호작용, 특히 가족상황 등에서 빚어지는 수많은 행동과 인식들이 연구대상이 된다. 그러나 주관적 관점은 사람들이 관찰하고, 알고, 실제로 행동한 사실들에 대하여 자기 스스로가 느낌, 희망, 기대 등을 가지고 있다는 것을 기초로 한다. 이러한 주관성은 어려운 이론에 의해서라기 보다는 단지 일상적으로 사람들이 "나는 무엇을 알고 있다", "나는 무엇을 좋아한다", "나는 어떤 일을 하면 즐거워"와 같은 평범한 진술로 표현될 수 있다. 그런데 이러한 주관성이 갖는 일상적인 생각들(notion)은 우연적이고 무작위적으로 존재하는 것이 아니라, 일정한 내적 구조(inner frame)를 가짐으로써 인간이 자신에 대하여, 또는 그가 과거에 어떻게 행동하였으며, 또 미래에 어떻게 행동할 것인가를 조정하고 선택하는 기초이며 지침이 된다. 이런 의미에서 주관성을 연구하는 것은 대단히 중요한 일이다. 주관성은 이미지 차원에서 연구될 수 있다. 여기서 이미지는 사람들의 마음속에 간직하고 있는 일상적인 개념, 느낌, 기대, 희망의 복합체를 의미한다. 그런데 연구자는 모든 개개인이 각인각색 다른 이미지를 가진다고 보지 않고 대상에 대한 이미지를 비슷하게 보유하는 집단을 찾으려 할 수 있을 것이다. 어떤 집단은 이미지상으로 광고보다는 소비 자체를 더 염두 해 둘 수 있으며, 또 다른 집단은 쇼핑을 가장 비중있게 생각하면서 소비와 광고는 이차적인 것으로 간주할수도 있다. 소비를 다른 요소보다 먼저 생각하는 집단도 있을 수 있다. 연구자가 이같이 소비, 쇼핑, 광고 등을 집단적 이미지 차원에서 조사한다고 하는 것은 사람들이 가지고 있는 일상적 이미지가 가지는 내적구조에 의하여 몇 가지로 대표되는 이미지 유형을 찾을 수 있음을 의미한다. 문체는 이 같은 주관성에 대한 고찰을 좀 더 체계적으로 정리하여 검증 가능한 형태로 나타내는 데 있다. 이 연구에서는 Q 방법론에 따라 주관적 이미지들을 Q-Sorts에 의하여 모형화하고 구조적으로 짜인 Q-Sorts에 의하여 이론을 검증할 것이다(Stephenson, 1953).

Stephenson은 그동안 인간행위 자체나 광고에 대한 연구가 커뮤니케이션 만족 개념에서 다루지 못한 점을 지적하면서, 유희이론적 접근의 필요성을 강조하였다(Stephenson, 1967). 특히 정치, 소비, 매스커뮤니케이션, 광고 등 새롭게 구성된 제도에는 유희적 요소가 지배적이며, 따라서 자아가 향상되는 자아 만족과 커뮤니케이션 만족을 기대할 수 있다는 것이다. 이것은 교육기관이나 정부, 종교, 군대조직과 같이 이미 틀이 잡힌 제도에서는 사회의 선을 위해 사람들이 일(work)을 하며, 여기에는 자아의 상실을 수반하기 때문에 커뮤니케이션 고통(communication-pain)이 따른다는 것이다. 그러니까 커뮤니케이션 고통은 일에서 나타나는 특징이며, 반대로 커뮤니케이션 만족은 유희(play)에서 발생하는 특징인 것이다.

유희에는 수렴적 선택성(convergent selectivity)의 원리가 작용된다. 이것은 사회적 통제(social control)와는 달리, 인간행위에 있어서 선택의 개별성을 지향하며, 이때 행위는 자발적이다. 즉, 모든 것이 개별성과 독립적 존재를 지향한다는 것이 수렴적 선택성의 원리이다.

이 같은 원리는 소비행위에 있어서도 나타난다. 치약, 화장품, 변비약, 화장지, 소화제, 자동차 등 자신의 수입 중 재량으로 쓸 수 있는 상품의 구입 시, 구매자는 마치 특권을 발휘하듯 사회적인 가치통제에서 벗어나 스스로 원하는 상품을 마음대로 구할 수 있음을 느낀다(Stephenson, 1970, p.11).

욕구(wants)의 개념은 커뮤니케이션 만족과 수렴적 선택성의 원리 중 빼놓을 수 없는 부분이다. 왜냐하면 소비자의 욕구란 자아가 고양되는 커뮤니케이션 만족의 범주에 들기 때문이다. 이것은 필요(needs)와는 상반된 개념으로, 기호, 유행, 패션, 취미와 같은 것이다. 사람들은 살기 위해 음식이 필요(needs)하지만, 그가 스테이크를 원하는(wants)

것은 자신이 고기를 좋아하기 때문이다. 따라서 욕구는 새로운 유행을 부추기는 요인이 되며, 자신을 위해 무엇인가를 소유하고 싶은 욕망이지, 무엇을 가져야만 하는 필수적인 것은 아니다(Knight, 1965).

Galbraith(1958)는 wants를 소비자들이 풍부한 제품들을 소비하도록 고안된 것이라고 주장하였다. 사람들은 정말로 필요하지도 않은 물건을 살 때도 있다. needs는 기본적인 것이고, wants는 인위적인 것이다. wants는 현대 사회의 소비를 유발하는 원동력이며, 소비행위는 wanta와 관련하여 일반화될 수 있다(선우동훈, 1991). Stephenson은 이러한 wants를 해롭거나 낭비적인 것으로 간주하지 않고, 오히려 자아를 고양시키며 발전시키는 것으로 보았다.[21] 수렴적 선택성은 사람들로 하여금 자유스럽게 자신들을 표현할 수 있도록 만들어 만족을 가져다주기 때문이다.

그러나 종교나 교육기관과 같은 사회는 보건, 교육, 안보 등과 같은 인간의 필요를 제공하기 위해 안정성을

---

21) Stephenson, 1971~1972.

요구하며, 이때 개별성은 인정되지 않고, 커뮤니케이션 고통을 경험하게 된다. 모든 사회적 통제와 윤리는 커뮤니케이션 고통과 연관되어 있다.

이상의 논의를 정리해 보면, 소비행위란 커뮤니케이션 만족과 수렴적 선택성의 개념으로 접근해야 하며, 소비자의 needs가 아니라 wants의 영역 속에서 다루어져야 함을 알 수 있다. 따라서 소비자의 주관적 의견을 체계적으로 접근할 수 있는 이론과 방법론이 요청되며, 이를 통해 스키마타(schemata)를 이해할 수 있을 것이다.

그런데, 여기에서 교육학용어사전에서 언급되는 '주관성[主觀性, subjectivity]'의 의미는 개인의 독특한 사적(私的) 경험을 반영하는 성질이며, 타인이 확인할 수 없는 개인의 경험을 의미하기도 해서 편파적이거나 비과학적인 뜻으로도 사용되는 경우가 있다. 주관적 경험도 여러 개인 사이에 일치를 보게 되면 문화적으로 객관성을 띠게 된다. 사회적으로 합의(合意)되었다고 해서 반드시 진리라고 말할 수는 없지만 사회적으로는 그것이 진실인 것으로 받아들여진다.

다음으로, 사회학사전에서는 다음과 같이 서술되어 있다. 객관성을 결여한 개인의 시각을 말한다. 이 용어에 대한 범위는 본질적으로 논쟁적인 문제를 가지고 있다. 실증주의 사회학에서 편향된 관찰이나 방법론을 비판하기 위하여 이 용어가 종종 사용되고 있다. 또 다른 극단에서는 해석학에서 주관성을, 사회학적인 것에 대한 이론화의 시도를 유일하게 가능하게 하는 방법으로서 긍정적으로 받아들이고 있다. 주관성이 바람직하지 않은 것인가, 또는 피할 수 없는 것인가에 대한 해답은 구체적인 세계에 대한 인간의 관계의 특성에 대한 존재론적, 인식론적 전제에 의존한다. 실제로 두 용어는 연속체의 양극을 말하며, 주관성과 객관성은 정도의 차이를 말하는 것으로 사용되고 있다. 주관성은 객관적으로 구성되고 그 역도 성립하지만(파슨스(Parsons), 알튀세르(Althusser), 기든스(Giddens)), 이분법은 쉽게 사라지지 않고 있다.

이에 반해, 객관성[客觀性, objectivity ; Gegenständ lichkeit(독일어), objectivité(프랑스어)]의 의미는 첫째, 주관성(主觀

性)의 반대로서 의식(意識)의 대상이 되는 사물·사건·관념 등이 가지고 있는 속성(屬性) 중에서 그 대상을 의식하는 사람의 영향을 전혀 받지 않는 성질. 즉, 개인의 주관(主觀)으로부터 완전히 독립되어 있는 성질을 통칭하는 말이다. 그러나, 이렇게 정의되는 「객관성」이라는 것은 의식하는 주관과 전혀 관계가 없으므로, 우리는 그런 성질이 있다는 것을 확인할 도리가 없다. 그래서 우리는 보통 누가 의식하더라도 변하지 않는 성질, 즉 모든 사람들이 공동으로 확인할 수 있고 공통주관적으로 인식된 성질을 편의상 객관성이라고 부른다.

둘째, (2) 성격특질(性格特質, personality traits)들 중의 하나를 가리키는 심리학적 용어. 주변의 상황이나 자신의 일시적 기분에 좌우되지 않고 사물을 있는 그대로 관찰하는 것을 뜻한다.

다시 말해서, 우리는 편의상 '간주관성'을 약한 의미의 객관성이라 하고, '실재적 객관성'을 강한 의미의 객관성이라 부르고자 한다. 임마누엘 칸트가 우리는 현상의 세계에 대해서는 확실한 지식을 가질 수 있지만, 사물 자체의 세계에 대해서는 알 수 없다고 했을 때, 그는 약한 의미의 객관성을 이야기하고 있었던 것이다. 반면에 현상과 실재를 구별할 필요가 없다고 보는 입장에서는, 과학적 지식의 객관성은 실재적 객관성과 다른 것이 아니다.

어느 경우의 객관성이든 객관성은 주관적 경험이나 확신의 느낌과는 구별된다. 객관성의 특징은 반복적 실험이 가능해야 한다는 데 있다. 아무리 개인적 혹은 집단적 확신감이 강할지라도, 그것은 결코 어떤 주장을 정당화할 수 없다. 아무리 의심할 수 없는 자명한 확신도 과학의 근거를 마련해주지는 못한다. 나의 확신감이 강했느냐 아니면 약했느냐, 자명하냐 아니냐, 저항할 수 없을 정도로 강력한 인상으로부터 왔느냐 아니면 의심쩍은 추측인가 하는 것은 과학적 진술들이 어떻게 정당화될 수 있는가 하는 문제와는 아무런 관련이 없다.

 [생각해 봅시다!]

* 여러분은 '주관성'과 '객관성'을 어떻게 구별하여 이야기 할 수 있습니까?

8. Q 방법론의 설계

William Stephenson은 과학에 있어 경시되어왔던 주관적 영역을 매우 중요시했으며, 그가 창안한 Q 방법론은 그동안 불가능하거나 비실용적이었다고 믿어왔던 주관적 행위를 매우 객관적으로 연구할 수 있는 바탕을 마련하였다고 할 수 있다.

Stephenson은 자연현상에는 가치의 구조가 개입되지 않지만, 사회 안에서의 인간은 특수한 의미와 적합성의 구조를 갖고 있기 때문에 인간의 주관성을 배제하여서는 인간의 본질과 사회현상을 제대로 볼 수 없다고 했다. 그는 주관성이 갖는 일상적인 생각들은 우연적이고 무작위적으로 존재하는 것이 아니라, 일정한 내적 구조를 가짐으로써 인간이 자신에 대해 그리고 과거에 어떻게 행동하였으며,

또 미래에 어떻게 행동할 것인가를 조정하고 선택하는 기초이자 지침이 된다고 보았다.

Stephenson의 주관성 강조는 Q 방법론의 기초 이론이 되고 있는 커뮤니케이션 유희 이론과 수렴적 선택성의 개념에서 뚜렷이 볼 수 있다. Stephenson은 커뮤니케이션을 일(work)의 개념을 수반하는 커뮤니케이션 고통(pain)과 유희(play)의 개념을 수반하는 커뮤니케이션 만족(pleasure)이라는 두 가지 측면으로 나누고, 전자는 사회적 통제가 작용하며, 후자는 수렴적 선택성이 작용한다고 주장한다.

사회적 통제란 비자발적 범주의 강요의 관점으로부터 문화가 기능하는 방법으로 동조, 합의 확고한 관습을 유도해내며, 한편으로는 그러한 문화적 결과로써 나타나기도 한다. 이러한 사회적 통제의 전형적인 예는 여론형성이다. 한편 수렴적 선택성은 새롭고 비관습적인 행동의 유형으로, 우리가 스스로 즐기고, 사회적 통제로부터 일정 정도 자유를 누릴 수 있는 기회들을 부여한다. 소비 행위는 수렴적 선택성의 원리가 작용하는 전형적인 예라 할 수 있다.

Stephenson이 명시적으로 제시하고 있지는 않지만, 사회적 통제란 '보편성'이 중요한 요소로 게재되어 있다고 할 수 있다. 이와는 달리 수렴적 선택성이란 다수의 일치된 견해 또는 합의를 지향하는 것이 아니라, 개별자의 자유로운 선택, 즉 개별적인 특수성을 강조한다. 이렇게 볼 때, 매스커뮤니케이션 행위의 사회통제적 측면은 자유가 아니라 억압이며, 개별적인 특수성이 아니라 보편성이며, 개인이 아니라 전체 지향적이라는 것을 의미한다. 반대로 매스커뮤니케이션의 선택적 측면은 통제나 억압이 아니라 자유이며, 전체가 아니라 개인이며, 일반적인 법칙이 아니라 특수성을 지향하는 것이다. 또 전자를 객관성이라고 한다면, 후자는 주관성을 의미한다(임상원, 1988).

Stephenson은 기존의 커뮤니케이션 현상에서 중요시되어온 신념, 가치, 믿음, 지위 모두가 사회적 통제이며, 물질적 득실에 치중한 것이라고 비판하고, 대부분의 사람들에게 실제 커뮤니케이션이란 그 자체가 재미있고 취향적이고 일상생활에서 벗어난 자유로운 자기표현으로서, 유희 성격이 더욱 강하다고 주장한다. 따라서 커뮤니케이션 결과는 의견의 형성이나 가치 혹은 태도의 변화라기보다는 수렴적 선택성에 의거한 자기 고양이 된다는 것이다.

Stephenson이 커뮤니케이션을 이렇게 놀이 또는 유희로 파악하는 시각에는 그의 '주관성(subjectivity)', 즉 인간 각자의 개별성 또는 특수성 개념이 깔려 있다고 이해할 수 있다. 이러한 입장에서 스티븐슨은 사회적 현실이 이미 구성된 것이 아니라 의미적으로 구성되는 것이며, 이러한 사회적 현실을 파악하기 위해서는 의미의 해석을 통한 이해의 방법이 필요하다고 본다.

따라서 그의 Q 방법론은 '외부로부터 설명'하는 방법이 아니라 '내부로부터 이해'하는 접근 방법을 의미한다. 이것은 Q 방법론이 연구자의 조작적 정의(operation definition)가 아닌, 응답자 스스로 그들의 의견과 의미를 만들어가는 조작적 정의의 개념을 채택하고 있는 가장 중요한 근거가 된다. 즉, 연구자의 가정이 아니라 행위자의 관점에서부터 Q 방법론이 시작된다. 따라서 여기에 사용되는 진술문(Q-statement)은 모두 응답자의 자아 참조적(self-referent) 의견 항목으로 구성되어 있다.

Q 방법론이 인간의 주관적인 속성인 선호, 이상, 아름다움, 취향 등을 측정한 것이라면, 기존의 R 방법론은 예컨대 수리능력, 언어능력, 지능과 같은 객관적 속성에 관한 것이다(Brown, 1980). Q와 R의 차이를 통계학적으로 설명한다면, R에서의 변인은 측정항목이나 자극(stimuli)인데 반해, Q에서의 변인은 '사람(person)'이라는 점이다(김홍규, 1990).

따라서 Q 방법론은 요인분석(factor analysis)의 하나이지만, 분석의 기본단위가 '사람', 즉 인간이란 점, 그리고 인간의 주관성이라는 점에서 여타의 통계방법과 근본적으로 구별되는 것이다. Q 방법론에서 한 현상이란 전체적 반응(시각, 생각, 이미지 등)이며, 이것은 주관적이기에 쪼개서 분석할 수 없는 것이다. 따라서 Q 방법론의 본질은 분석적 접근만을 통해서는 이해할 수 없는 인간의 총체성을 강조하는 정신이 내재해 있는 것이다.

    Stephenson은 경험주의 방법론이 갖는 한계와 오류를 극복하기 위한 이해의 방법으로 Q 방법론을 주창하고 있지만, 해석학이나 현상학에서 제시하는 것처럼 다소 애매모호하고 주관적인(신비적인) 해석방법과는 거리를 두고 있다. 즉, 해석학에서의 간주관성(intersubjectivity), 감정이입과 추체험, 그리고 현상학에서의 초월과 환원의 방법은 객관적 근거를 갖지 못하고 주관적인 해석에 머무를 수 있다는 문제점을 Q 방법론은 concourse 이론 1)과 요인분석 등을 통해 최소화시키고 있다(김홍규, 1990).

 [생각해 봅시다!]

* Q와 유희적 해석, 그리고 커뮤니케이션과는 어떠한 의미로 다가올 수 있습니까?

9. Q 방법론의 적용과 이해

　Q 방법론 프로그램은 QUANAL과 CENSORT 두 종류가 있는데, QUANAL 프로그램은 강제분류방법을 통해 수집된 데이터만을 분석하도록 만들어진 반면, CENSORT 프로그램은 강제분류방법과 비강제분류방법을 통해 수집된 데이터를 분석할 수 있다. QUANAL과 CENSORT는 프로그램을 작성하고 실행하는 방법에 차이가 다소 있지만, 분석결과는 거의 차이가 없다. 따라서 Q문항 분류방법에 따라 연구자가 사용하기 편리한 프로그램을 선택하여 사용하면 된다.

　다음은 'Q'를 적용하고 이해하는 9가지 방식을 소개하고자 한다. 아마도 Q를 처음 배우고 적용하는 학도들에게 도움이 될 것으로 생각한다.

첫 번째, Q 방법론의 소개된 근원적인 문제를 살펴보면, 객관주의 과학에서 대부분 무시되고 있는 주관성을 탐구하는 객관적 방법을 제시하기 위해 개발되었다. 인간의 개인적 또는 집단적인 능력이나 행동을 연구하기보다는 개인의 주관적 심리, 태도 등 주로 내적 관점에 대해 연구하려고 하는 의도였다.

두 번째, 개념적 차원에서 살펴보면, 연구대상의 특정변인을 규정하고 그 변인을 대표하는 진술문을 수집 또는 작성하여, 그 특정 변인의 구조에 적하하다고 여겨지는 적은 대상자로 하여금 진술문을 대상자가 주관적으로 정한 기준에 따라 정상 또는 준정상분포(Quasi-normal distribution)가 되도록 분류하게 하고, 이를 상관분석, 변량분석, 요인분석과 요인정렬의 순서로 통계처리 하는 방법이다.

세 번째, Q는 사회현상 및 인간의 심리, 태도, 인식에 대한 주관적 조작적 정의와 개념화, 유형화, 서로 다른 인식의 차이, 이해관계자 간의 의견 조정을 위한 유형을 확인하고, 설명하는데 매우 유용한 목적을 지닌다.

네 번째, Q원리상, 개념구성, 응답자의 주관적 반응에 대한 개인 군집 발견, 개인 간의 반응에 대해 상관관계를 분석하여 비슷한 개인들은 군집하여 유형화, 군집분석, 변인으로부터 요인 추출하는 요인분석, 요인배열 후 연구자가 명명화(naming)를 이끌어 준다.

다섯 번째, Q 방법론의 과정을 다음의 8가지로 구분해 볼 수 있다.

① 변수정의
② 진술문 수집/작성: 변인을 대표하는 진술문 작성
③ 대상자 선정: 준비된 진술문에 반응할 사람 선택
④ 정규분포 분류: 대상자로 하여금 준비된 진술문을 정규분포(준정상분포)가 되도록 분류(Q 분류에 의해 강제분류), 평균분석과 유목평균분석
⑤ 상관관계 분석: 대상자가 분류한 결과를 보고 분류한 사람들 간의 상관관계 계수 산출

⑥ 요인분석: 상관관계 행렬을 요인분석하여 요인추출
⑦ 요인해석: 추출된 요인을 바탕으로 요인정렬 및 해석
⑧ 주관성 분류: 변인과 진술문에 대한 대상자의 주관성 분류

여섯 번째, Q연구를 함으로써 다음의 장점과 한계점을 제기할 수 있다.
① 장점: 개인에 대한 연구, 탐색적 연구에 기여, 주관적 진술에 대한 객관적 분석 등
② 한계: 관찰의 1회성, 비확률표집과 적은 표본으로 인한 대표성 및 결과의 일반화, Q 분류 시 진술문의 강제분류(7단계 이상)로 인해 신뢰성 저하 및 연구 대상자의 자연스러운 반응 제한 등

일곱 번째, Q 연구의 적용 측면에서는 다음의 3가지 차원을 제시할 수 있다.
① 개인의 태도와 심리 및 사회문화적 현상들에 대해서 군집과 유형화 연구

② 다양한 학습내용과 프로그램의 효과와 유형화 평가
③ 한 변인의 개념 및 구성 내용의 연구

여덟 번째, Q 연구의 이해 차원에서 보면, 우선, 인간의 주관성(subjectivity)을 체계적으로, 엄밀한 수량적 방법으로 연구함으로써 독특한 심리측정학적 원리를 포함하고 있는 방법이라고 할 수 있다. 또한 Q 방법론은 개인의 주관적 인식에 초점을 맞추어 어떤 대상이나 현상에 대한 개인들의 총괄적인 인식의 모습을 자세히, 그리고 보다 객관적인 방법을 통해서 도출해 내는 조사방법으로 그 특징은 한마디로 조작적 주관성(operant subjectivity)이다. 이는 어떤 정의나 개념을 미리 가정하지 않는 대신, 조사대상자들이 진술문을 분류하는 행동을 해석하고 그 의미를 조사대상자의 주관적 인식으로 해석하는 것이다. Q 방법론은 행위자의 관점에서 출발하여 주관성의 구조에 따라 형성된 유형을 발견하고 각 유형에 대한 이해와 설명이 가능하기 때문이다. 또한 Q 방법론은 전통적인 개념인 '변인 간의 상관' 대신에 '사람 간의 상관'을 탐색함으로써 사람 간의 유사성 및 유형을 찾아보려는 데 목적이 있다.

아홉 번째, Q의 특성은 6가지로 정리해 볼 수 있다.
① 관점: 주관성
② 대상: 소규모 개인(30명 이내)
③ 방법: 질적방법과 양적방법의 통합
④ 초점: 기존 양적연구에서의 변인과 변인의 관계가 아닌 사람과 변인과의 관계
⑤ 과정: Q 표본 - P 표본 - Q 분류 - 자료분석
⑥ 활용: 개념화, 설문지 개발, 유형화, 군집분석

[생각해 봅시다!]

* 여러분은 Q 방법론을 적용하여 어떠한 가능성을 이해하였습니까?

10. Q와 R의 차이점과 장단점

Q 방법론은 주관성을 과학적으로 측정하는데 효용이 있다. 인간의 주관성은 입증하기 쉽지 않지만, 주관성은 일정한 구조와 형태를 띠고 있다. 연구를 위하여 주관성의 구조와 형태를 측정하는 데에 Q 방법론의 효용성이 있다.[22] 또한 이 연구방법은 주관성의 과학화에 기초를 제공한 일종의 철학적, 심리적, 통계적, 그리고 계량심리적 도구이다. Q 방법론의 우수한 장점은 인간행위의 주관적인 면, 즉 인간의 주관성의 관찰과 측정에 있다. 주관성이라 함은 동적인 상황 속에서 자결적(Operantly)으로 정의되는 개인의 관점 및 관념을 말한다.[23]

---

[22] Brown, S.(1980). Political Subjectivity : Applications of Q Methodology. New Haven: Yale University Press. 참조

[23] 김순은(1997). "지방자치의 발전을 저해하는 요인분석: Q 방법론의 적용", 〈정책분석평가학회보〉. 7(1). p.6.

다음은 Q와 R의 비교한 표이다.

	Q 방법론	R 방법론
모집단	일련의 진술문	일련의 사람
변인	일련의 모든 진술문에 반응하는 것	사람의 어떤 특성
변인의 상호작용	상호작용한다	상호작용하지 않는다
전이조건	개인 내 차	개인 간 차
점수분포	준 정상분포 이룸	정상 또는 준 정상분포 이루지 않음

Q방법이 갖는 장점은 다음과 같다.

첫째, 계산이 편리하다. Stephenson은 테스트 간의 상관계수를 산출하는 R 방법과 Q방법 간에는 방법상으로 큰 차가 있는데, 그 무엇보다 중요한 차이는 Q방법이 R 방법보다 계산이 간편하다는 것이다.

둘째, 개인 내 항상성을 측정할 수 있다. 개인의 태도에 대한 내적 항상성 측정은 쉬운 것이 아니다. 그것이 가능하다면 중요한 예측적인 것을 측정할 수 있다. 태도측정에 있어서 어떠한 척도를 사용해서도 그것을 재는 것은 쉽지 않다. 그러나 Q분류는 개인 내 항상성 계산을 간단하게 측정할 수 있다.

셋째, 이론검증의 접근방법이다. 이론 혹은 이론의 검증측면을 유목으로 표현할 수 있고, 유목을 표현하는 문항을 구할 수 있다면 Q방법은 이론검증에 강력한 방법이 될 수 있다.

넷째, 개인에 대해 집중적으로 연구하는 데 적합하다. 교육이나 기타 프로그램의 영향에 의한 개인의 태도변화 또는 개인의 자아에 대한 인식 변화를 연구할 경우에, Q진술문을 여러 번 Q분류하게 하고 그 변화에 대하여 집중적 그리고 심도 있게 연구할 수 있다. Q분류자료는 일상적인 임상연구나 사례연구의 장점을 활용해서 객관적으로 분석할 수 있다.

다섯째, Q방법은 탐색직 연구에 기여할 수 있다. Q방법은 새로운 개념이나 가설을 발견할 때 유용하다.

여섯째, 복잡한 종속변인에 대한 독립변인의 효과를

검증하는 데 사용될 수 있다.

일곱째, 요인분석과 요인배열의 통계적 유용성을 갖는다. Q분류는 정밀한 조작에 의해 개인의 양적 특징의 열거에 유용하며, 같은 특징을 지닌 사람들간의 차이를 비교할 수 있다(김헌수 외, 2000, pp.130~131).

Q방법이 갖는 단점은 다음과 같다.

첫째, Q방법은 대체적으로 소표집이나 개인 대상 연구에 적합하다. 따라서 대표집이나 횡단적 연구를 수행하는 데 어려움이 따르기 때문에 연구결과를 일반화하는 것이 어렵다.

둘째, Q방법이 갖고 있는 통계적 문제로서 대부분의 통계적 검증은 각 문항에 대한 반응자의 반응이 서로 독립적임을 가정한다. 그러나 Q방법은 일정한 수의 진술문을 강제적으로 정상분포나 준정상분포에 배치하도록 요구되기 때문에 독립성 가정에 위배된다. 그러나 진술문의 수를 증가시키거나 유의도 수준의 값을 높게 책정한다면 그런 문제점은 사라질 것이라는 주장도 있다.

셋째, Q방법의 중요한 절차 중 하나인 Q분류가 강제로 선택되어 분류된다는 것이 문제점으로 지적되고 있다. 즉 분포에 맞게 진술문들을 분류하기 때문에 반응자들이 이에 맞추기 위해 비합리적으로 진술문들을 분류하기도 하고, 자연스럽게 사고하기 어려울 수도 있다. 그러나 강제선택을 하기 때문에 연구가 타당하지 않다고 말할 수는 없다(박도순, 2003, p.413).

[생각해 봅시다!]

* Q와 R의 공통점, 차이점, 활용성에 대해서 논의하여 봅시다.

11. 맺음말 : Q의 연구 및 발전 방향

　Q 방법론은 기존의 과학에서 간과하여 왔던 인간의 주관성(subjectivity)을 과학의 대상으로 포함시켜 이를 전혀 새로운 방법으로 탐구하고 이해하는 것으로서 그 동안 객관과 주관, 혹은 설명과 이해 그리고 양적분석과 질적분석이라는 대립적 전통을 통합하는 새로운 방법론이라 할 수 있다. 자연 세계를 연구하는 방법론으로는 가치가 개입되고 한 사회 안에서의 인간이 갖는 특수한 의미와 적합성의 구조를 연구할 수 없기 때문에, 인간과 사회를 연구하는 새로운 방법론(패러다임)으로 Q 방법론이 등장하게 되었다. 이처럼 인간의 주관성을 배제해서는 인간의 본질과 사회현상을 제대로 연구할 수 없다는 과학적 신념에서 Q 방법론이 시작되었으며 실로 많은 영역에 걸쳐 적용

가능성이 검증되고 그 유용성 또한 입증되고 있다.

Q 방법론은 1960년대 국내에 소개되었으나 소수 특정 학자들에 의해서 연구가 간헐적으로 이루어져 체계적으로 발전하지 못하다가 최근 계량적 방법론에 대한 회의와 한계로 인한 대안적 방법론의 탐색이 활발해짐에 따라 주목을 받기 시작했다.

이에 한국주관성연구학회를 비롯하여 앞으로 보다 적극적인 학술발표는 물론 Q 방법론의 올바른 이해와 적용 가능성의 범위를 넓힐 기회를 마련하는 계기가 마련되었으면 한다. 또한 국제주관성연구학회(ISSSS)와 공동으로 국제 학술 교류를 가져 국내 Q 연구자들에게 다양한 연구를 유도하고, 다양한 전공분야와의 융합 연계 연구가 다각적으로 취급되기를 기대한다.

 [생각해 봅시다!]

* 향후, Q의 발전을 위해 필요한 사항은 무엇입니까?

【부 록】

1. Q-sort instructions for any Q-sample

2. Brown summarizes the comparisons he makes between Q and R methodologies, further underscoring their methodological differences.

1.
Q-sort instructions for any Q-sample

1. Q-SORT INSTRUCTIONS for any Q-Sample

GENERAL REMARKS:

About any sufficiently complex issue, condition, or situation, everyone is likely to hold many 'opinions', or have a wide array of 'feelings', some pro and some con, and some neutral or in between.

A **Q-sample** provides a sample of all such statements of 'opinion' or 'feeling' about a given issue, condition, or situation.

Q-sorting is a method which represents (or models) these 'opinions' or 'feelings' in a statistical manner. It is based on one of the two great methods of classical experimental psychology, the method of **impression** (the other is the method of **expression**). The concern in Q-sorting is always with matters of **impression**, of **opinion**, **judgement**, **value**, **belief**, and the like, and not with matters of **fact**.

The **instructions** given below are for a Q-sample of size $n=48$, with the following 'forced' distribution of scores:

Scores	−5	−4	−3	−2	−1	0	+1	+2	+3	+4	+5
Frequency	3	4	4	5	5	6	5	5	4	4	3

$(n=48)$

(The instructions are adaptable to any other integer scale and Q-sample size.)

/

INSTRUCTIONS:

The **sorting** is best performed on a large table on which place-cards (3"x5") are spread out in a wide array, each card indicating the score and the number of statements required for that score, as follows:

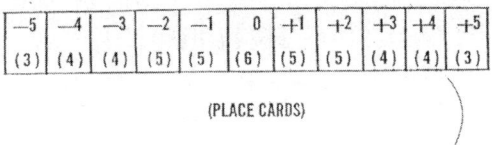

−5	−4	−3	−2	−1	0	+1	+2	+3	+4	+5
(3)	(4)	(4)	(5)	(5)	(6)	(5)	(5)	(4)	(4)	(3)

(PLACE CARDS)

The Q-sorting is performed on the table in front of these place cards. When it is completed, the 48 statements will be lying face-up, in their forced distribution, as follows:

(PLACE CARDS)

−5	−4	−3	−2	−1	0	+1	+2	+3	+4	+5
(3)	(4)	(4)	(5)	(5)	(6)	(5)	(5)	(4)	(4)	(3)

(48 statements)

CONDITION OF INSTRUCTION.

The condition under which the Q-sorting is performed is always as follows:

"*You are asked to use the statements to represent what matters most to you, positively or negatively. Use the statements to describe your 'opinion' or your 'position', or 'views' about the substance of the statements. Those that you feel strongly about, or that you value most positively are given score +5. Those you feel strongly about, but negatively, are given score —5. Those statements about which you have no feelings, or about which you are neutral score at or near zero (0). If you do not know what a statement means, it should be scored 0.*"

METHOD: THREE PILES FIRST

First shuffle the pack of 48 statements to randomize them. They are then read through by the subject, who begins the Q-sorting by sorting them into three broad piles, one at the **right for pro** statements (about which he feels positively on some degree), one at the **left for con** (about which he feels negatively in some degree), and one in the middle for the neutral, doubtful, ambiguous, or meaningless statements.

There should be about the same number of statements in each pile.

NEXT: TO-AND-FRO SORTING

The Q-Sorting continues with the following to-and-fro procedure:

"*Choose the 3 from the pro pile with which you are most strongly in agreement, i.e. about which you feel most strongly positively. Place these face-up in front of the +5 place-card.*"

"*Now choose the 3 from the con pile with which you most strongly disagree, i.e. about which you feel most strongly negatively. Place these face-up in front of the —5 place-card*".

"*Now move back to the pro pile and choose the 4 with which you are next most in agreement. Place these in front of the +4 place-card.*"

"*Then move to the con pile and choose the 4 with which you are next most in disagreement. Place these in front of the —4 place-card.*"

The subject continues in this manner, alternating from right to left as he approaches the middle of the scale.

When finished, all 48 statements will be lying in front of the place-cards: the subject can read them all at a glance; he can of course change the position of any that he wishes to, at any point in the Q-sorting. The object is to have a Q-sort that represents the subject's 'opinion', or feeling', or 'overview', no matter how he performs it -- the above to-and-fro is recommended as most practical, and reliable, but the subject can do it anyway he likes.

SCORING:

Each statement's number is entered on the score sheet on the appropriate cell which indicates the score it received. (A separate score sheet is provided.)

INSTRUCTIONS FOR ADMINISTERING Q SORTS

Before attempting to administer a Q sort to someone else, you should perform the sort yourself. This will alert you to the kinds of problems the subjects will encounter and will help you in administering the sorts.

First, prepare a deck of 3 x 5 index cards to contain the following: one card with DISAGREE written on it, one card with AGREE, and one card with NEUTRAL/UNCERTAIN; and one card for each of those presented below:

#1	#2	#3	#4	#5	#6	#7	#8	#9
2	3	5	7	8	7	5	3	2

and,

#1	#2	#3	#4	#5	#6	#7	#8	#9
2	4	6	6	7	6	6	4	2

Write, don't type, the information on cards; typewriting is too small for the purpose.

Preliminary Instructions:

Before presenting the Q deck to the subject, some preliminary comments are in order:

1. Explain that one deck contains statements about Ichord, and one deck about Hearnes.

2. Explain that we are interested in their opinions about the candidates. This is not a test--there are no right or wrong answers. Their opinions are all that matter.

3. Explain that you are going to ask them to sort the statements according to how much they agree or disagree with them. Tell them that they can change the placement of any statement at any time.

Conducting the Sort

4. Place the DISAGREE card in front of the subject and to the left, the NEUTRAL card in the middle, and the AGREE card to the right.

5. Ask the subject to read each statement and put the statement on one of the three cards in front of him. If he agrees, the card should be placed on the AGREE card. This procedure is called the Pre-Sort.

6. When the Pre-Sort is completed, pick up the AGREE statement pile and put the others aside. Place the cards marked #7, 8 and 9 on the table, in order, with #9 on the right.

7. Ask the subject to read through the AGREE statements and pick the two statements he agrees with the most. These should be placed on the #9 card.

8. From the remaining AGREE statements, pick the three statements he agrees with the most and place on the #8 card. (note that the Hearnes and Ichord distributions are not the same; one calls for three statements on #8 and one for 4).

9. Have the subject continue sorting statements from the AGREE pile until he runs out.

10. Pick up the DISAGREE pile. Place the remaining numbered cards in front of the subject, left to right, beginning with #1.

11. Tell the subject to read through the DISAGREE statements and pick the two that he disagrees with the most. Place them on card #1.

12. Continue sorting statements from the DISAGREE pile, always sorting for DISAGREEMENT, until you run out of statements.

13. Give the NEUTRAL pile to the subject. Have the subject pick up where he left off when sorting for AGREEMENT. For example, suppose the subject stopped with four statements in the #6 pile. Since #6 calls for 7 statements, we need three more to complete #6. Have the subject pick the three he most AGREES with and place them on #6.

14. Continue sorting for most AGREE until all of the statements have been sorted.

15. Put the numbered index card on top of each pile. Pick up the piles in order, left to right. #1 will be on top, #9 on bottom. Put a rubber band on the deck and prepare to do the second Q sort.

16. When you get home, fill in the statement numbers from the statements on the distribution form. The two statements from the #1 pile are to be recorded in the boxes under #1. Order within the column is unimportant.

17. Please make a mental note on the Pre-Sort. The number of statements in the AGREE and DISAGREE piles should be nearly the same; if they are not, we need to know it. Please indicate which column number (i.e., #4,5...9) the subject's last AGREE statement fell in.

18. Should anyone ask about the numbers on the statements, simply tell them the truth--the numbers are merely for identification.

19. Naturally, we guarantee the anonymity of the subjects' responses.

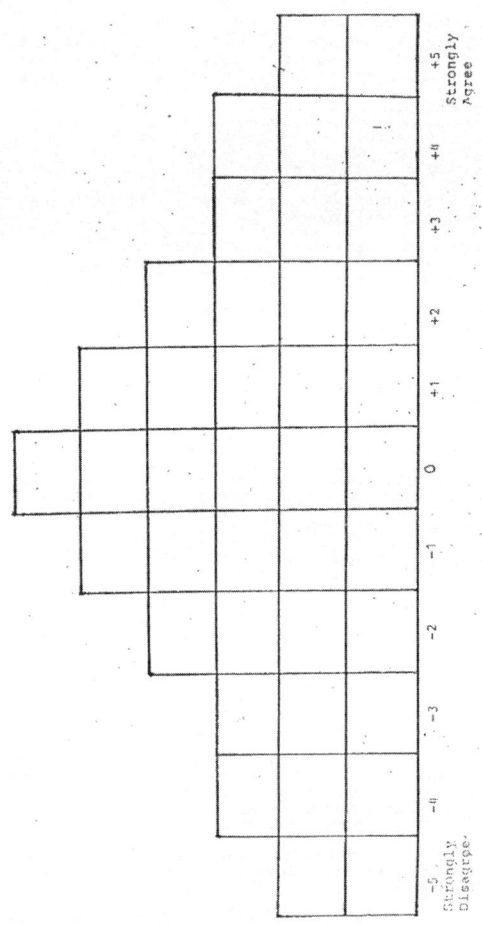

UNIVERSITY OF MISSOURI
COLUMBIA

SCHOOL OF JOURNALISM

AREA CODE: 314
449-4185

SORTING INSTRUCTIONS

The enclosed deck of cards contain statements about journalism research. I want you to sort these statements into piles according to whether you agree or disagree with them. You'll find this easiest to do at your desk or at a table.

1. Remove the rubber band from the deck and pick up the three gold cards. Arrange them in front of you like this:

                  −   ?   +

2. Put the 11 blue cards aside for now and pick up the white cards.

3. Read each statement and then put it on one of the three gold cards according to whether you agree or disagree with the statement. Place the statements that you agree with on the (+) card. Place the statements that you disagree with on the (−) card. Place statements that you feel neutral toward or can't make up your mind about on the (?) card.

   Feel free to change the placement of the statements at any time. Ignore the small number in the upper left corner of the statement cards--it is merely for identification.

4. When you've finished dividing the statements into the three piles pick up the blue cards. Spread them out in front of you, left to right, from 1 to 11, as follows:

   #1   2   3   4   5   6   7   8   9   10   11

   The idea is that when you finish the sort you will have 11 piles of statement cards--one pile for each blue card. The small number in parentheses on each blue card indicates how many statement cards you should wind up with in that pile. For example, you should place 2 statements on card #1, 3 on card #2, etc.

5. Pick up the right hand pile (+) of cards that you have sorted. These are statements that you agreed with. From this pile, pick the 2 statements that you most agree with and place them on Card #11. From the remaining cards for the (+) pile, pick the 3 statements you most agree with and place them on Card #10.

   Continue selecting statements that you most agree with and placing them on card numbers until you run out of statements from the original agree (+) pile.

   Remember that you may change the placement of a statement at any time.

6. Pick up the left hand pile (-) of cards you previously sorted. These are statements that you disagreed with. From these statements, pick the 2 that you <u>most disagree</u> with and place them on card #1. From the remaining cards in the (-) pile, pick the 3 statements you <u>most disagree</u> with and place them on card #2.

   Continue selecting statements you <u>most disagree</u> with and placing them on card numbers until you run out of statements from the original disagree (-) pile.

7. Pick up the original middle (?) pile of cards. These are statements that you felt neutral or undecided about.

   Begin sorting these statements at the point where you ran out of statements from the (+) pile when you were moving right to left from card #11.

   For example, let's say that you ran out of statements from the (+) pile when you got to card #8. In fact, let's say you ended up with only 3 statements to place on card #8. Card #8 calls for 6 statements, so you need to pick the 3 statements from the (?) pile that you <u>most agree</u> with to finish out card #8.

   Then continue on to the next blue card, etc., sorting for <u>most agree</u>, until all of the cards have been sorted and placed.

8. Now pick up the statements on card #1. Record the identification number (upper left corner) for each statement in the space below and comment briefly why you selected each statement. Do the same thing for the statements on card #11.

   Comments on Card #1.

   Statement no. ___

   Statement no. ___

   Comments on Card #11.

   Statement no. ___

   Statement no. ___

9. Now, pick up card pile #11, blue card and all, and place it on top of card pile #10. Pick up the combined pile and place it on top of card pile #9. Continue on down the line. Put a rubber band around the final pile. That's it.

10. Put the cards and the questionnaire in the return envelope and mail as soon as possible.

    Again, thank you very much for your cooperation.

On Interpretation of Q Factors

In interpreting Q factors, one tries to bring to bear all the information and insight he can to unlock the psyche of the Q factor, or hypothetical person represented by the factor. The process of interpretation is primarily abductive. That is, one seeks an "answer" or "explanation" that accounts for the particular distribution of statements.

Interpretation involves not only finding explanations but also communicating those explanations. One interprets data for some audience or audiences and it is useful to keep the audience in mind during the interpretation process.

A frequent criticism of Q studies is that the interpretation is subjective. Indeed, it is common procedure in many studies, particularly theses and dissertations, to point out that the explanation presented is merely one of many that could have been presented and to invite the reader to make his own interpretation. The data, of course, are not subjective; the arrays of statements representing factors are mathematically arrived at based on the operations of respondents. The experimenter has little idea of and no control over what the factors will be. Thus, the subjective part of interpreting Q data is not in the combinatorial activity, but in explaining the combinations. Such subjectivity, however, is severly limited by the fact that the Q researcher must follow these basic "rules" in interpreting Q factors:

1. the explanation must fit the data.
2. the explanation should be the simplest, most likely explanation.
3. the explanation should not contradict other data.
4. the explanation should be internally consistent: the placement of each item in the array should be accounted for by the explanation, with no contradictions permitted.
5. in short, the explanation must make sense.

Interpretation of Q factors is a highly creative process. Jerome Bruner (On Knowing: Essays for the Left Hand) has defined creativity as an act that produces "a shock of recognition following which there is no longer astonishment." Normally, one spends a great deal of time searching for the explanation; he is confronted with confusion, uncertainty, contradiction. Finally, the shock of recognition comes--the explanation is obvious. The only astonishing thing at such a point is that you didn't see the explanation immediately, it is so obvious.

I. Interpreting Q data.

   A. What is a Q factor, and what does it represent?

   Q factors are operant combinations of "like" people, i.e., combinations of people who have sorted items in similar, correlated, ways. The people are linked together by common beliefs, attitudes, opinions. A Q factor array represents a hypothetical attitude, the "common" attitude of the persons on the factor. The arrays are weighted according to each person's loading on the factor. It is useful to conceive of a Q factor as being a person, instead of a collectivity of persons. Thus, it is possible to describe "him" or to ask questions of the nature, "what is he really like?" It is also easier for the reader to think in terms of a "him" or "her" than an "it." The higher a person's factor loading, the more like the hypothetical person he is and thus should you encounter someone who has a loading of .800 or greater it may be useful to think of him as being very representative of the factor, and to pay particular attention to his comments, his demographic information and the like.

   B. Interpretation Input

   1. Theory.
   2. Demographic data.
   3. Questionnaire data.
   4. Comments on extreme items in the Q sort.
   5. Q sorts and Q factor arrays. This may include analysis of structured Q samples.

   It is important to not only discuss what a Q factor is like in its attitude, but also to discuss what kinds of people make up that factor, or type. Thus, after completing the factoring/rotating phase and having determined who is on which factor, compile a working summary sheet of the people on each factor. One can do this via a cross-tabulation process with SPSS, or by merely separating his questionnaire. Look to the demographic information for insight in interpreting the Q arrays. Otherwise, such information is used almost entirely in a descriptive manner. It normally will be true that persons will not cluster together on factors according to any demographic variable background, but one should always check for that unusual finding.

   Comments on extreme items are used in essentially three ways. First, to get a better idea of the person's viewpoint--to see what it is about the statement that he is reacting to, instead of relying on assumption. Second, to gain insights into why the person sorted the statements in the manner he did. It would be ideal, of course, to have a person give a comment on every statement, but such is neither practical nor perhaps valid. Third, to provide forceful ammunition for the written report of the interpretation. From a writing standpoint, using these direct quotations is like adding flesh to bones.

The WRAP phase (Weighted Rotational Analytical Procedure) of
QUANL provides several types of factor arrays, each based on
standard (z) scores. Specifically:

    a. factor array for each Q factor, or type. This is, you will note,
the Q sort for the hypothetical person.

    b. factor array of the paired differences between factors (i.e.,
difference between I and II, I and III, etc.). This array is
found by subtracting one factor's standard score on a given
item from the other factor's standard score on the same item.
The items are then arrayed from greatest positive to greatest
negative. That is, if the array is for Factor I and II, the
positive end of the array will include those statements that
Factor I rated higher than Factor II; those at the other end
of the array will be those that Factor II rated higher than
Factor I. Note that many of the items showing large differences
will be those that basically were rated neutral by one factor.
Note too that such a direct comparision is possible only with
standard scores.

    The value of this array is in showing how factors <u>differ</u>.
Keep in mind that because the difference might be <u>great</u> (say, 2.00)
does not necessarily mean that Factor I agrees strongly with the
statement: it merely means he agrees with it considerably more than
does Factor II.

    c. factor arrays showing how one factor compares with "all others."
To obtain this array, one compares one factor with the average
of the other factors. One should be careful in using this array;
it makes sense only when the factors being averaged are fairly
similar.

    d. Consensus items. These are items that have been scores approximately
the same by all factors. More specifically, we normally stipulate
that the factor scores be within 1.00 standard scores.

    Consensus items are particulary valuable in communication research.
They indicate the common ground, the common denominators. These
are the things that everyone likes, dislikes, or is neutral about.
In some studies, you might be only interested in the consensus items,
particulary, for example, if you had to launch a campaign that
had to be aimed at a broad cross-section of an audience instead of
at highly defined segments.

C. The Process of Interpretation.

    Each factor represents a puzzle. Solving the puzzle is usually
difficult, always time-consuming. Interpretation demands that the
experimenter take bold, creative leaps, that he look not only at
the obvious (such as a statement's standard score) but also at the
complex (such as the strange combination of several statements taken
together, apparently in contradiction). It requires patience, insight,
and an abductive mental framework. You will know when you've done
your job well when you experience Bruner's "shock of recognition."

Normalized Factor Scores for R' Factor

Body Segment	Scores
25 Total height	3.934
11 Arm (center of collarbone to fingertip)	1.492
19 Leg (length from inseam to ankle)	1.136
17 Thigh (length from widest part of hips to knee)	0.331
7 Shoulders (width)	0.254
18 Shin (from knee to ankle)	0.253
8 Trunk (center of collarbone to navel)	0.211
16 Hips (widest part)	0.176
9 Chest (width)	0.039
10 Waist (at narrowest part)	-0.021
12 Forearm (elbow to wrist)	-0.132
24 Foot (length, heel to toe)	-0.167
1 Head (length)	-0.281
13 Hand (wrist to fingertip)	-0.352
20 Thigh (width)	-0.405
2 Head (width at eye-brow)	-0.511
22 Calf (width)	-0.557
6 Neck (width)	-0.557
21 Knee (width)	-0.557
15 Palm (width)	-0.610
23 Ankle (width)	-0.674
14 Wrist (width)	-0.706
5 Mouth (width)	-0.730
3 Eyes (distance between)	-0.775
4 Nose (distance across base)	-0.791

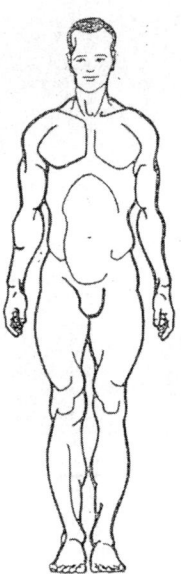

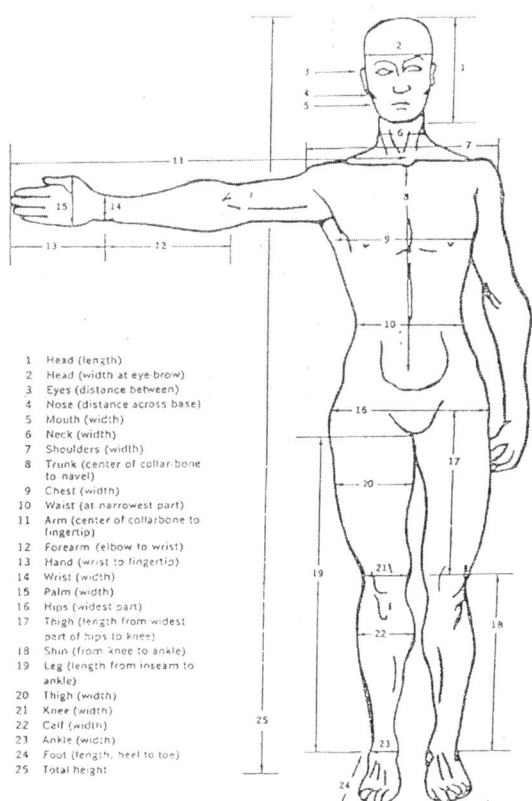

1. Head (length)
2. Head (width at eye-brow)
3. Eyes (distance between)
4. Nose (distance across base)
5. Mouth (width)
6. Neck (width)
7. Shoulders (width)
8. Trunk (center of collar-bone to navel)
9. Chest (width)
10. Waist (at narrowest part)
11. Arm (center of collarbone to fingertip)
12. Forearm (elbow to wrist)
13. Hand (wrist to fingertip)
14. Wrist (width)
15. Palm (width)
16. Hips (widest part)
17. Thigh (length from widest part of hips to knee)
18. Shin (from knee to ankle)
19. Leg (length from inseam to ankle)
20. Thigh (width)
21. Knee (width)
22. Calf (width)
23. Ankle (width)
24. Foot (length, heel to toe)
25. Total height

2.

Brown summarizes the comparisons he makes between Q and R methodologies, further underscoring their methodological differences.

2. Brown summarizes the comparisons he makes between Q and R methodologies, further underscoring their methodological differences

> Large numbers of persons are nowhere at issue since differences are among factor types...,rather than categorical aggregates; types, in turn, are operantly defined by subjects' behaviors and are therefore in contrast to the social categories (class, party, sex, etc.) intrinsic to R, but which have logical status only.
>
> In Q, factor analysis can...play an inductive or abductive role, but relationships can...be reversed--i.e. explanations of theories can be expressed in variance designs and propositions can be tested factor-analytically: For example, a Q sample can be structured around Jung's (1923) theory of introversion-extraversion as a possible explanation of social perception; the proposition that "introverts would prefer to be extraverts," however, is not contained in the Q-sample structure, but is tested by asking an introvert to describe himself and his ideal self, and then showing, via factor analysis, that the two are orthogonal, the latter being extraverted (Brown and Hendrick, 1971).
>
> R focuses on tendencies and potentialities that hold true across individuals and situations (e.g., an alienation scale always measures alienation in every context), whereas Q is more directed toward concrete situations and the single case. Statistically, this concrete-general distinction is manifested in the R-methodological acceptance of simple structure and varimax criteria in factor analysis, a body of rules assumed to be applicable in any and all situations, as opposed to the Q-methodological reliance on judgmental rotation, which is guided by the requirements of the specific problem under scrutiny.
>
> In sum, R and Q...are more often supplementary than complementary, each providing an angle on human behavior that is missing in the other. The irreducible difference is that R provides a perspective on behavior that is external, i.e., from the observer's standpoint: the subject, after all, is unaware that the test he is taking is a measure of alienation; he merely receives a score. In contrast, Q provides a perspective on behavior that is internal, i.e., from the subject's standpoint: The investigator, after all, does not know which statements are valued most until the subject places them under the +5; rather than receiving a score...,the subject _assigns_ a score, and this makes all the difference.

Sampling in Q Methodology requires more attention than it does in most studies of human behavior, not only because of differences in philosophy and purpose but also because of practical considerations. The sampling of stimuli will be discussed in this chapter and the sampling of people will follow in the succeeding chapter.

A casual review of scholarly literature will show that most researchers exercise great care in the sampling of people. Considerable attention is paid to gathering samples of adequate size and representativeness. Elegant statistical procedures are used to assess the extent of probable sampling error. It is quite uncommon, however, to find many studies in which the same concern has been paid to the sampling of stimuli. In Q Methodology, the sampling of stimulus items is of primary importance, particularly when the testing of theory is at issue.

It will be remembered from earlier chapters that the concern in Q is with the person, individually or collectively. The object in stimulus sampling is to provide the individual with a selection of meaningful "things" that he can order in some way so as to provide a model of what he thinks. The concern is not with the stimulus items per se but with the opportunities they provide individuals to express their subjectivity.

Before proceeding to a discussion of sampling rules and procedures, it will be useful to define terms used in Q sampling.

Much confusion about Q has resulted from the frequent misuse (or complete misunderstanding) of terms carefully spelled out by Stephenson. If readers remember nothing else from this book, it is hoped that they will remember that Q sample and Q sort are not synonymous terms--they refer to completely different parts of Q Methodology.

Item. A stimulus item is one of the many "things," usually statements typed on index cards, to be sorted.

Q Population. A Q population is the collection of items gathered for a Q study.

Q Sample. A Q sample is a selection of items taken from a Q population.

Q Sorting. Q sorting is a process by which an individual sorts through the Q sample and assigns each item a score.

Q Sort. A Q sort is the result of Q sorting. A Q sort is a model of an inidvidual's subjectivity.

Structured Q Sample. A structured Q sample is a selection of items constructed by design according to specified dependencies.

Unstructured Q Sample. An unstructured Q sample is a set of items selected without attention to specified dependencies.

P Population. A P population is the collection of people available as subjects.

P Sample. A P sample is a selection of people taken from a P population.

It can readily be seen, then, that data gathering in Q consists of sampling persons from a population and asking them to sort through and score a sampling of items from a collection of such stimuli.

Stimulus Items

Almost any class of things can serve as items. For the moment we need to be concerned only with two principles: first, it should be possible to manually manipulate the items--to move them about and "sort" through" them; second, the items should be "self-referent" to the sorters, that is, things about which they can express an opinion.

Most frequently items are statements printed on 3 x 5 index cards. Numerous other items could be used. Stephenson's initial exploration involved merely the use of sheets of paper in different colors.[1] Photographs frequently are used. In journalism research it is by now common to use brief news stories, news story "lead" paragraphs, news story ideas, and even headlines. Instead of photographs, one could use the items pictured--such as vases, paintings and the like. Names of people, or their titles (e.g., minister, physician, baker, etc.) have been used. Several studies have been conducted using printed advertisements. Editors could use copies of publications, layout "dummies," or mock layouts to determine reader preferences in design. Television ads could readily be sorted now that home-use video-tape recorders are becoming commonplace. Why not a sample of wines, of perfumes, of books?

Sampling Background

Obviously, the physical properties of some of these items and the cost of acquiring them would limit their use. Just as obviously, there is a rich universe of items that readily lend themselves to Q.

The selection of persons/samples is a well-defined and well-understood process. Elementary textbooks on research methods include a section in which the basic process is set forth: the investigator defines a population (say, all women majoring in physics at the University of Missouri), obtains a population list, and then systematically selects some members of the population to constitute the sample. The selection process is conducted in such a way as to attempt to guarantee that only "chance" has operated and selection bias has been minimized. The process is completed with the calculation of the standard error, which reports how much probable error in selection may have occurred. The concern, ultimately, is to make inferences about the population based on information obtained from the sample.

It is a neat, even elegant, model that has served science well. There is just one little problem: in practice, sampling doesn't quite work the way it's supposed to. We do not wish to scrap standard sampling methods; rather, we wish merely to remind readers of what they are--models. Sampling models provide plans of action and means by which we can evaluate the "goodness of fit" of the sample with the population; they do not provide reality. Except in small-sample cases, pure random samples rarely exist outside the laboratory!*

A brief discussion of some of the problems inherent in persons sampling should provide useful background for the understanding of Q sampling.

The first step in sampling is to define the population. Using the previous example (women physics majors), the next step is to obtain a list of all the members of the population, which is easily achieved because the chairman of the department is well-organized (she's already compiled such a list) and is eager to help (she, too, is a researcher).

It is an easy matter to devise a system whereby each woman on the list has an equal chance of selection. If the list were short, we might simply write the names on slips of paper, put them in a box, shake thoroughly, and draw n slips. If the list were long, we might resort to a table of random numbers. Having selected a sample, we are ready to begin data-gathering. We first decide to contact subjects by telephone. Rather quickly we find that many telephone numbers (copied from the list) are inaccurate. Many calls are made, few answers are obtained. Because we work at the pizza palace Monday, Wednesday and Friday nights and our classes occupy the day-time hours, we make our calls on Tuesday and Thursday nights and during the weekends. Despite our every effort

---

*By definition, a sample is random if, and only if, each item (person/place/thing) in the population has an equal chance of selection.

there will be some women we will never contact (perhaps they have no telephone, they've moved, they've dropped out of school, they're not home on just the nights we call, etc.). The point is that some members of the sample have no chance of taking part in the study and some have a much greater chance of selection than the others. Whether the sample will be hopelessly biased (is there something systematically different between the women who were contacted and those who weren't?) is a matter of serious concern, but in any event the study can make no claim for having a random sample.

The physics majors example was chosen specifically to illustrate the pitfalls that can occur even when an apparently good population list is available. Fortunately (or unfortunately, for the naive sampler), there is no shortage of population lists available for many studies. Consider only a few: telephone directories, city directories, voter registration lists, utility company users, newspaper subscribers, personal property and real estate tax lists, club membership lists. You no doubt can think of many more. The common problem with most population lists is that they are out-of-date. In a highly mobile society, certain lists (particularly telephone and city directories) are 10 to 20 per cent inaccurate before they come off the printing press. Telephone lists are suspect for two additional reasons: upward of 10 per cent of all residential phones are "unlisted," and the trend is increasing, and a surprising number (perhaps an additional 10-15 per cent) are inoperative at a given time.[2] Stories about voter registration lists are almost legion--addresses that don't exist, buildings that never were, people long-since dead. This is not to suggest the abandonment of lists. Indeed, by using two or more such lists and cross-checking them many sampling problems can be avoided.

Consider, finally, the problems encountered when no population lists are available. A common procedure is to sample areas, or units within areas. For example, a pollster might be given a map of city blocks, selected at random, and then be instructed to stop at the third house on the right from a specified intersection. The interviewer would proceed to stop at every third house, perhaps going all the way around the block. Instructions might include alternating between male and female occupants. Unfortunately, most interviewing will have to be done in the daylight or early evening hours. There will be some areas where it will be difficult to find interviewers willing to go.

16

Ingenious samplers have devised many techniques to minimize problems, such as the creation of randomly generated telephone numbers to overcome the problem of unlisted numbers.

In the sampling of persons, then, two major limitations can be observed: first, the <u>selection</u> of individuals may be less than perfect--some people may have a greater chance of selection than others, while some may have no chance of selection.

Second, the <u>participation</u> in the study by individuals may be inadequate--although the names were randomly selected, it was impossible to contact the individuals, or, once contacted, they refused to participate.

Virtually all "real world" studies fall victim, to some degree, to one or both of these sampling limitations. Fortunately, there is no need to throw all such studies out. Instead of asking whether the sample fits the model, scientists instead ask, "Does the sample fit the model <u>adequately enough for the matters at hand</u>?"

The models are there to guide the researcher, to make him aware of the potential pitfalls, to make him aware of his own selection biases and to make him think seriously about the systematic gathering of data. More than just a good faith effort is required; the researcher is expected to exercise every skill at his command and, finally, to carefully explain procedures used so that others can evaluate, criticize, and attempt to replicate.

The danger in sampling comes not in the failure to fit the model but in failing to realize when the fit is grossly inadequate. It is of no great concern, for example, that some members of the population have no chance of selection. What matters is if the members participating in the study are systematically different from those who do.

Perhaps the best example, because of the massiveness of the undertaking, of the sampling model gone awry is the decennial effort to survey the people of the United States. The objective is not to conduct a survey by sampling but to conduct a census--by definition, a study in which each member of the population is studied. Although virtual armies of interviewers are hired, vast sums of money are expended, and each citizen is required by law to answer the questions, the U.S. Bureau of the Census fails at conducting a census, or even a good survey sampling. The reasons are numberous--"transitional" people (itinerant workers, families moving, etc.), people unwilling to admit to the crowded conditions in which they live, illegal aliens, for example--but the fact remains that the census aactually accounts for only about 90 percent of the population. That, of course, makes it one huge sample (about 200 million), but a sample nonetheless. Lest one find comfort in reasoning that a sample so large in numbers and percentage of the population couldn't be far off, it is important to note that the primary reason millions of people drop through the cracks is most assuredly because those people were <u>systematically different</u> from the ones contacted.

To summarize, the sampling model so prevalent in the behavioral and social sciences is one that rarely is found to work perfectly in the empirical world. The intent in providing this background was not to denigrate R methodology nor to provide the foundation for something new and different in Q Methodology. Rather, it has been to remind the reader that the concern is with a <u>model</u>, not with something akin to a natural law. As those who have designed studies well know, sampling is not a cut-and-dried undertaking. The pragmatic concern is, "Does it work?" It does, indeed--for the purposes at hand.

Selecting Q Samples

The sampling of stimulus items in Q Methodology is similar to the more familiar sampling of persons. Samples are selected from identifiable parent populations. Many of the same procedures are used and many of the same principles apply. Because the focus is on persons instead of tests, however, there is little concern for making inferences about the population of items.

Q samples are of two types: structured and unstructured. They will be dealt with separately because they differ in both selection procedures and purpose. The discussion will deal primarily with statements as items, with occasional reference to other kinds of stimuli.

Unstructured Q samples

Unstructured Q samples usually are used when the primary purpose is to identify, describe, and explain types of people, or when the researcher is not ready to posit specific theoretical ideas. An advertiser, for example, might want to segment a potential market to determine what types of people would be most interested in a new product. A politician might want to determine what kinds of campaign appeals would work with specific types of voters. Structured Q samples usually are used when the primary purpose is the testing of a specific theory.

In unstructured Q samples the procedure is more one of constructing a sample than it is of selecting it. The situation is comparable to the sampling of persons in survey research where no population list is available. The survey researcher can resort to other means when population lists are unavailable--such as instructing interviewers to go to specified housing units (e.g., the third house on the right hand side of the street). The Q sampler has no such alternativaes. A population list must be made. It is not merely a matter of defining a population; quite literally it is a matter of constructing the population (of physically gathering statements on index cards, or photographs, or vases, or wine bottles).

The first step is to define the population. Suppose that we want to study attitudes about wine and wine-drinking. The purpose is a very practical one: to sell more wine. Q Methodology is particularly appropriate for such a study. Not only will the potential market be segmented into types of people, but the interpretation of those types will provide specific ideas and symbols to guide the preparation of advertising and marketing strategies to sell the wine. The population definition would be: "all self-referent statements about wine."

Although "self-referent" has been discussed previously, it is worth repeating. A self-referent statement is a statement of opinion, as opposed to a statement of fact, that the subject can project onto. It is a statement of fact that "California is a major producer of wine." It is a statement of opinion that "California wine is as good as any produced in France." We are not testing the person's knowledge of wines; we are providing an opportunity for him to describe his attitude about wines. Statements of fact merely lead to "right" or "wrong" answers. In Q there are no right or wrong answers--only opinions.

In constructing the population the objective is to acquire every available statement [or item]. Any source is fair game. Where does one look for statements about wine, or about anything else? One thing is certain: wherever we find statements about wine we are not likely to find many of them in one place. The sampling of items will not be accomplished easily and quickly.

An obvious starting point is literature produced by wine distributors. Not only would this likely help in gathering statements but it likely will help the researcher acquire a better understanding of wine. Gather a collection of magazines and scan them for advertisements for wine. A trip to the library will quickly produce a list of books and articles about wine. Newspapers may run stories. In other words, the Q sampler needs to be reminded that in the vineyards of science, it is not only the scholarly literature that can provide vintage stimuli. Consider movies ("The Days of Wine and Roses"), poems, the Bible (Psalms 104:15--"wine that maketh glad the heart of man"), songs. In short, consider any source that has to do with wine.

For most studies where statements will serve as items, the best source will be interviews. Given that the eventual objective is to determine people's opinions and attitudes, there is an obvious logic involved in starting with people and their opinions. The interviews are conducted along lines suggested by Merton, Rogers and others. They should focus on the topic (wine, in the present example) and should be basically non-directive in approach. Productive interviews are not easy to conduct and the neophyte would be well-advised to study the available literature and then practice with family or friends before going into the field.

The interview would start with a simple explanation of the purpose: we're gathering statements to be used in a study of what people think about wine. The trick in such interviews, as most reporters quickly discover, is to get the person talking as freely as possible. The typical interview will start slowly, with the interviewer doing most of the talking. In a productive interview, the interviewee gradually will talk more freely and eventually will dominate the session. It usually is as hard to get interviewees to stop talking at the end as it was to start them talking at the beginning. Any number of techniques might be used to overcome the initial hesitancy of interviews. You might show them a magazine advertisement for wine, or ask them what they think is the "selling technique" behind television wine commercials they remember. You might bring bottles of wine and get them talking about labels. You might use the ploy, "someone told me yesterday that only snobs drink wine in restaurants"--what do you think? You could simply inquire about their own wine-drinking habits. Do they drink wine? How much? Do they prefer one brand over another? Why? The interviewer has to be a good listener. He has to be alert to comments and be ready to probe further.

Properly executed, the interview should procede in much the same fashion as the stereotypic psychiatrist-patient session. The psychiatrist sometimes has difficulty getting the patient started and thereafter merely nods or says sterling intellectual bonmots as "hmm," "I see," "very interesting," "could you explain that to me," and "when did you first notice." The technique is to get the subject talking and to keep them talking, so long as they don't stray too far from the topic. The strategy is to be as non-directive or neutral as possible; — people may quickly clam up if they suspect their views differ from the interviewer's, or that their views are "wrong." Occasionally, however, an interviewee may be so reluctant to talk freely that only a direct confrontation will elicit comment.

Good conversationalists usually make good interviewers, for they usually are good listeners. It is quite commonplace for interviewees to suggest that they really don't know much about the topic and that they don't see how their opinions could be of any help. You will find, rather quickly in fact, that people have opinions about everything, although they may never have realized it. Take advantage of the fact that people love to talk about themselves and their opinions--when they see that they have a respeactful audience. People are genuinely flattered to be asked their opinions...and most are happy to help. Like the psychiatric session, the well-conducted interview has a therapeutic effect on the participant. People enjoy it.

The matter of note-taking requires some consideration. The beginner will find it best to use a simple cassette tape recorder. This will free the interviewer to concentrate entirely on orchestrating the interview. It also provides a means by which the interviewer can study and improve his technique. The proficient interviewer may want to use a recorder as a backup but to rely primarily on writing down statements as they are made, taking care to avoid distracting the interviewee in the process.

The interview ends when the interviewee's supply of self-referent statements appears exhausted. After conducting a couple of sessions, the interviewer will come to recognize a pattern: relatively few useful statements will come at the beginning, followed by a flurry of good statements, ending with a gradual decline. The same pattern will generally be found for the interviews as a group. As the interviewer develops in skill and knowledge of the topic the number of useful statements will increase sharply after the first couple of interviews and then decline steadily. Thus, it is remarkably easy to know when you've done enough interviews. After surprisingly few interviews, the point will be reached when few or no new statements are obtained. To be on the safe side, conduct one or two additional interviews. If these prove fruitless, it is time to stop.

The number of interviews needed varies from study to study. The investigator must be guided by the pattern that develops during the interviews. Surprisingly, 10 to 12 interviews will normally suffice, assuming that they are well conducted and attention is paid to the selection of interviewees. In selecting persons to interview it is important to remember our purpose: to obtain as many statements about the topic as we can. There is no concern with such matters as how many times a particular statement is uttered, or what is the most frequently made statement. A random selection of subjects to interview is self-defeating. By definition a random selection of people is most likely to produce a representative sample, which, in turn, will likely include only the most typical or common statements. To find the unusual, or even rare, statements--to effectively complete the task of constructing the population--a systematic effort must be made to find people likely to hold different opinions. This is not as difficult as it may at first seem. Of particular value are people who have special interest or expertise in the topic. If wine is the topic, wine company representatives and salesmen, wine store operators, professional wine tasters, and the like would make good subjects. So would grape growers, restaurant managers, and members of gourmet dining groups. If the focus of the study were somewhat different, we might well want to also consider "winos," police officers, members of Alcoholics Anonymous, and physicians. It likewise is useful to find naive subjects--people who apparently know little about the topic. Such people are likely to have very rich images and normally are easy to interview, perhaps because, once having stated their ignorance, they don't feel threatened. On many topics, and wine surely is one of them, it would be helpful to consider age of the interviewees. In short, it is necessary to be creative and deliberately seek out persons who are likely to hold different opinions.

Before turning to the business of selecting which statements will be used for the Q sample, it is important to reflect on the process to this point. Systematically, we have tried various means at our disposal to put together a complete population list. It would be folly to suggest that literally every statement about wine has been obtained, but we should feel rather confident that we have come close. Certainly all major themes should now be represented.

Preparing the Statements

Do not attempt to record each statement every time you come across it in your search. Because we have no interest in how many times a statement occurred, it is necessary to record it only once. Likewise, don't bother with statements that are extremely similar to ones already recorded. Consequently, you will be very busy recording statements in early interviews and very "unbusy" in later ones. Statements should be typed on index cards after each day's work (it is tedious work and if left to pile up will drain your enthusiasm for completing the task). Merely typing many statements on a sheet of paper will greatly impede the sampling (or winnowing) process that lies ahead.

Attention is turned next to "cleaning up" the statements. The experienced Q sampler will have been doing this from the start, but the beginner likely will find it easier to do at the final stages of constructing the population list. To prepare the cards for final sampling we need to check the following:

(1.) Items should be homogeneous as to class. All items should have reference to the study topic.

(2.) Items should be self-referent. A good test is: can the word "I" be inserted?

(3.) Statements should be edited for the subjects who will sort them. Different audiences require different complexity levels. Pay particular attention to vocabulary--avoid difficult or uncommon words that subjects might not understand. Statements should be conversational in nature but should follow proper grammatical rules.

(4.) Statements normally should express a single idea, unless the purpose is to force the subject to make a comparison. For example, the statement "I like to serve wine at parties because it impresses my guests and it's more convenient than mixed drinks," normally would be split into two different statements. The subject may like to serve wine at parties but not because it's more convenient. At best, the statement is likely to end up with a neutral ranking; at worst, it will end up with an extreme negative ranking and the erroneous interpretation might be made that the subject doesn't like to serve wine at parties.

(5) Statements that are mere opposites or antonyms to others should be discarded. There is no need to include both these statements: "I like wine"; "I don't like wine." The subject can indicate whether or not he likes wine by placing one of those statements on the agree or disagree end of the continuum.

It should be obvious, having finished the cleaning-up operation, that most of the statements have been changed from their original form. Attribution of statements from either published materials or from interviews should be eliminated. Statements should not be enclosed by quotation marks. In some cases, there may be some value to the investigator at the factor interpretation stage in knowing where statements were obtained. If they came from a published source, the investigator might want to refer to the context for insights. If they came from an interview, the investigator might want to talk to the interviewee again.

At this point, normally a stack of several hundred edited cards will remain. Two options are available in choosing the final Q sample: select a simpel random sample or select a systematic sample according to themes.

Selecting a random sample clearly is the easiest and quickest procedure. There are several advantages in selecting such a sample: it would be the easiest and quickest procedure, it would most closely approximate standard models for sampling, and it would minimize possible selection bias by the investigator.

For now, assume that a sample of N = 50 is desired. Any system that would guarantee that each card has an equal chance of selection will suffice. The cards might be numbered 001 to N, and a table of random numbers might be used to select 50 cards. The cards might simply be shuffled thoroughly, "cut" as one would do playing poker with playing cards, and the first card dealt would be selected for the Q sample. Fifty such cuts would complete the sampling.

Utilization of random sampling results in two disadvantages: an unnecessarily arbitrary decision must be made about sample size and important information about the nature of the Q population is ignored.

In Q methodology, the size of the Q sample is determined by statistical, reliability, and convenience requirements. Once again, it is important to recall that Q is an ipsative procedure, involving intra-individual significances instead of inter-individual differences. Too few items will so reduce the amount of information to be gained that it will be difficult to extract distinctive factors and to make meaningful interpretations of their differences. Too many items will drastically reduce the reliability of the Q sample. How many items are too few or too many depends primarily on the complexity of the items themselves and on the demands placed on the Q-sorter.

Photographs are relatively simplistic; subjects can quickly and easily sort through them in a consistent (that is, reliable) manner. Names are even less complex. Statements can be simple ("I like wine") or complex ("In selecting a wine, I like to experiment, satisfy my curiosity, and develop a new taste"). Some items, in other words, can be sorted quickly but others will require the subject to pause and contemplate about "me." Consider a sample of introspective statements,

such as Stephenson put to "Rogers" to test theories stemming from
Freud's classic analysis of "Dorax":[3]
- "I have great faith in many of my own ideas."
- "I seldom overtly react against the tastes of others even if they appear crude to me."
- "I think of myself as being compliant and obliging--ready to do whatever I am asked to do."
- "I often feel that people around me are acting according to false ideals."

Such statements will not be dismissed by the subject with a simple "I agree" or "I like that"; rather, the subject will pause and reflect, "Am I like that?" and "Is that what I do?" Clearly, it is a mistake to assume that subjects can sort complex items as quickly, easily, and reliably as simple items.

The sorting task also varies when other demands on the subject are difficult or unusual. For example, suppose the condition of instruction were to sort the items according to the way you think your mother, spouse, best friend, or boss would, or how you would if you were your "ideal self," or if you were working in your "ideal" job situation. Likewise, if the subject is asked to make repeated fine discriminations between items (that is, the distribution calls for relatively few items to be placed at each point along the continuum--the problem would be maximized if you asked the subject to rank order the items 1 through N). It is much easier to choose six statements you "agree with the most" than it is to choose only two statements.

The more complex the items and the greater the demands on the subject the more likely reliability will suffer. In most Q studies, subjects will require 30 minutes to an hour to complete one Q sort. Reliability--the consistent placing of statements in the same general order--begins to diminish as the length of the sorting operation increases.

The selection of the Q sample size will vary according to each study's unique attributes. Nonetheless, it is possible to offer some rule-of-thumb guidelines. In general, the Q sample should contain 40 to 60 items. Feel free to use 60 or more items when the stimuli are simplistic (photographs, names, "easy" statements). When stimuli are complex, the investigator should use smaller samples but probably should not drop below N = 30. Kerlinger[4] suggests that "a good range is from 60 to 90," and "that the number should probably be not less than 60 nor more than 140." Such large samples, however, almost surely will decrease reliability rather than increase it as Kerlinger implies. Sampling requirements in structured Q samples are somewhat different. In any case, Q sample reliability should be tested as a matter of course in each study.

A simple random sampling of the Q population, in short, leaves the investigator with no solid rationale for determining sample size. In such cases, it would be best to use the 40-60 rule-of-thumb.

The other disadvantage of random sampling of the Q population is that it is done "blindly"; that is, without any attention to the items themselves and to what has been learned in constructing the Q population. The investigator, having conducted an exhaustive (and probably exhausting) search of literature and folk lore and having interviewed people at-length, should know a great deal already about opinions, attitudes, beliefs, values and such about the topic. Such information can be put to good use in selecting a more precise measurement tool.

A systematic sample takes into account the statements and what has been learned. By now the statements have ben encountered several times: when first "discovered," via literature or interview searches, when recorded on cards, and probably two or three times when cleaning them up. Read through them again, but this time look for themes or categories. Another reading of the cards about wine might suggest several general groups of statements: taste, bottle label information, effect of drinking, self-enhancement, ("I enjoy introducing special friends to a favorite wine"), and others. Go through the cards again, only this time sort the statements into piles according to the themes suggested by the last reading. A "Miscellaneous" pile will be necessary for the many statements that won't fit a theme. Some statements, of course, will overlap theme categories; there is no need for concern unless several statements overlap the same theme category, in which case one chould consider combining the categories.

Go through the cards again, pile by pile. Do the themes "make sense?" "Are the cards more-or-less in the right piles?" If in doubt about the themes, ask someone else to go through all the cards (after you've carefully marked theme categories on the back) and to sort them into piles for any identifiable themes. Once confident about the theme sorting, go through each pile again and try to eliminate statements very similar in wording or meaning. Prune statements that create opposites. Look for opportunities to combine into one statement an idea expressed by two or more statements. Going through this final stage, you may think of new statements. Include them. The fact that the statement comes from you is irrelevant. The population, you will recall, was defined as all statements about.... You could easily have interviewed yourself as well as others.

The final stage in a systematic sample is to select statements from the categories. Options, again, are available. The simplest procedure would be to draw a random sample of statements from within each of the theme piles remaining. To add precision, it might be better to sample proportionately from each category. Thus, if 20 per cent of all the statements are in theme category A, 20 percent of the sample should come from that category. The reader should recognize immediately that the former process is similar to a stratified random sample and the latter procedure is similar to a stratified proportional random sample.

The other option in selecting the items is to select the statements that the investigator, for one reason or another, thinks best represent each theme. Such decisions take direct advantage of the information gained from the population construction process.

Once the statements have been selected they need to be checked for balance or valence. <u>Sort through the selected cards</u>, by theme category, <u>and determine</u> whether each statement is positive, <u>negative or neutral.</u> For example, "I like wine" is a positive statement, "Wine is too expensive" is negative, and "Consider wine by large firms. They have advantages small ones don't" is either neutral or hard to classify. Naturally, the statements you agree with are likely to be disagreed with by someone else, and vice versa. The point is that anyone should be able to sort through the statements and find approximately an equal number with which to agree or disagree. There should be some neutral statements in every Q sample, but <u>they should be considerably fewer</u> than the positive and negative ones. Thus, for a sample of 50, we might find about 21 positive, 21 negative and 8 neutral statements. The actual numbers will vary from study to study and are relatively unimportant. The essential consideration is that a significant number of both positive and negative statements be included and that they they exist in approximately equal numbers. In this sense, even unstructured Q samples are structured. It usually is an easy matter to balance the sample. In most cases simple editing (inserting a "don't" here, a "dislike" there) will suffice. In some instances it may be necessary to refer back to those statements discarded in the previous step to find ones that provide the desired balance. The balance should hold for both the sample as a whole and for each theme or category. Again, relative balance rather than perfect balance (don't be concerned about a 4-3 split within a category, for example) is the goal.

Pre-testing is the final step in the Q sampling process. Prepare the items for formal sorting. Statements should be neatly typed or printed. Photographs or illustrations should be mounted. Each item should be assigned a number, 1 through N. Using the formalized Q sample, ask someone to perform the Q sort according to the instructions to be used in the study. Observe the person during the process. Watch for changes in the sorting pattern: a long pause over a statement may indicate confusion, for example. Does the subject seem to understand the directionss? How long did it take to complete the sort? When the sort is complete, ask the pre-tester for comments, particularly about anything that was confusing or difficult. Reassemble the items and ask the subject to go over them again to make comments on those that proved troublesome. Based on the pre-sort, make necessary changes in the sample or instructions. If the sort took more than an hour, it will be necessary to decrease the sample still further (even a slow sorter should finish in less than an hour in most cases). Continue pre-testing, using different persons, until the problems appear to have been eliminated. Ideally, persons chosen to pre-test would be like those in the population who will do the eventual Q sorting. Their opinions and expertise about the topic are irrelevant; indeed, it is sometimes best to find naive subjects.

Finally, proceed to conduct reliability tests. A handful of persons, say two to six, should complete a Q sort and re-sort, preferably at different time intervals. That is, you might ask one person to do a re-sort immediately after completing the first sort and shuffling the cards, a second person might do the sorts a day apart, a third two days apart, a fourth a week apart, and so on. Compute correlation coefficients for each person's two sorts. Average the correlations obtained. A sort/re-sort correlation of about .30 is significant for a Q sample of 50 but considerably more stringent demands should be placed on the data. As was discussed in chapter ___, because of statistical limitations inherent in the methodology, it is essential that Q investigators be ultra-conservative in the selection of significance levels. If the average correlation for the reliability testers is below .50, something is definitely amiss and further work is needed to refine the sample or the instructions. In general, one should try to determine why any individual's sort/re-sort correlation fell .

below .50. Normally, individual reliability coefficients will be considerably higher, with scores in the .70s and .80s most prevalent. Another important reason for insisting on high correlations is, of course, that the amount of explainable variance increases as the correlation increases. A correlation of .80 provides nearly seven times as much explainable variance as one of .30 ($.80^2$ = .64, or 64 per cent of total variance, as opposed to $.30^2$ = .09).[*]

Structured Q Samples

Whereas the unstructured Q sample "starts from scratch" and proceeds more-or-less with regard to variables, structured Q samples start with theory and proceed to "tests" of the theory. It is Q Methodology's close affinity with theory, an inherent feature of structured Q samples, that has attracted the most acclaim and has secured its place in the study of behavior.

Before discussing how to develop such samples and the important philosophy of science principles involved, we will briefly describe what is meant by a structured sample.

In a structured Q sample, Fisherian experimental design principles are followed and specific variables of a theory or hypothesis are built

---

[*] For elaboration on this point, see Stephenson, Study, pp. 282-285, on how "specificity" variance relates to factor interpretations

---

into the selection of items. In other words, the items are partitioned in one or more ways. The simplest partitioning would involve two levels of a single variable. Even unstructured samples, it was noted, should be "structured" as to balance. Thus, "balance" would be the variable and the partitions would be "positive," "negative" and "neutral." For example, a sample of photographs might be structured according to whether they contained people or not. Each photograph would be classified "people" or "non-people." Theory, based on considreable prior research, would indicate that photographs with people are, in general, better liked than photographs without people.

Or, suppose two variables of two levels each were used to test advertising appeals. One variable would deal with "testimonials," the practice of having someone (frequently a well-known personality--Joe DiMaggio and his coffee ads quickly comes to mind)--or a "typical" person--(Mrs. Average Housewife is an all too-familiar character) proclaim the virtues of the product. The theme, of course, is "I use it and I recommend that you do too." The sample would thus be divided by Type of Advertising Appeal--(a) testimonial, (b) non-testimonial. There is reason to believe, however, that testimonials work better for some products than for others. Although there are many possibilities (of course, theory and the purpose of the study would be the deciding factors), we elect to simply add the two-level variable "Type of Product," which we partition into (c) men's products and (d) women's products. The design thus looks like this:

Type of Advertising Appeal

	Testimonial	Non-Testimonial
Women's	Cell 1	Cell 2

	A_1B_1	A_2B_2
Men's	Cell 3 A_2B_1	Cell 4 A_2B_2

Each advertisement to be included in the sample will be either a testimonial or a non-testimonial and each will have to be either for men's products or for women's products. Furthermore, half of the non-testimonials will be for men's products and half for women's. The design provides four (2 x 2) combinations of the variables: A_1B_1, A_2B_2, A_2B_1, A_2B_2. A balanced block design, one in which an equal number of items would represent each combination or "cell," thus would call for one-fourth of all the items to represent each combination. The design would be replicated several times; that is, additional examples of each combination would be found and included in the sample. Twelve such "sets" of the basic design probably would suffice and would provide 48 items (2 x 2 = 4 combinations x 12 = 48). To review quickly, 24 of the items would be testimonial and 24 would not; 24 would be for men's products and 24 would be for women's; 12 would be testimonials for women's products, 12 for testimonials for men's products, and so forth.

To determine whether testimonials were preferred to non-testimonials, the mean of Column 1 would be compared to the mean of Column 2. To determine whether men's products were preferred to women's products, the mean of Row 1 would be compared to the mean of Row 2. It may well be that the most interesting information will be found by looking at the interactions of the variables; that is, by comparing one cell mean to another. For example, compare the mean for Cell 1 (A_1B_1) with the mean for Cell 2 (A_2B_1).

Structured samples organize stimuli, control variables, and provide testing situations. In terms of the number of variables and number of levels employed, structured samples are limited only be feasibility and pragmatic concerns. As the number of combinations increases, fewer replications are possible and the chances for erroneous interpretations increase. It should be obvious that the number of combinations increases sharply with the addition of only one variable or level. For example, three variables with two levels each provide 8 combinations (2 x 2 x 2). Three variables with three levels each provide 27 combinations (3 x 3 x 3).

To structure a Q sample, as Kerlinger states, "one has perforce to enunciate some kind of theory." The structural variables and their interactions and independent variables. The investigator is formally designing an experiment in which the structural variables and their interactions are independent variables. That is, by merely selecting certain variables to include in the structure, the investigator has stated that there is reason to believe that these variables will have an effect on how items are sorted. Thus, the structural variables and their interactions are independent variables. Theories may be represented very formally or quite informally in the sample, but the mere existence of structure makes it obvious that theory is involved.

As subsequent examples should illustrate, rather complex theories can readily be structured into Q samples for direct testing. This capability was quickly noted by many after The Study of Behavior and has become standard practice for many Q investigators. Erlinger noted, "It (structured sampling) is one of Stephenson's most significant contributions to psychometric measurement and to psychological and educational research. Strange to say, this is the point that most investigators using Q have neglected, despite the fact that it is perhaps one of the most original and powerful contributions of Stephenson.(5)

As might be expected, the procedures are quite different than those used in unstructured sampling. Many of the same guidelines hold: the items should have class homogeneity; they should be self-referent, that is, synthetic propositions onto which people can project. The same "cleaning-up" procedures discussed earlier are applicable.

In the unstructured sample the concern was with drawing items more-or-less at random from a parent population, which had to be composed through literature searches, extensive interviews and the like. In structured samples the concern is with selecting items that "fit" the variables selected. Such items may be "found" or they may have to be "created."

One starts, perforce, with a theory, or a general explanation of what may be relevant to the intended purpose of the study. One could hardly find a better example than Stephenson's ingenious structuring of a sample to test Riesman's well-known theory of social character.(6) Riesman defined three types of social character: inner-directed, other-directed and tradition-directed. Inner-directed people are dependent upon inner beliefs and confidence in themselves. Other-directed people look to other people for support in developing attitudes and behavior. Tradition-directed individuals are dependent upon the traditions of the society and its institutions, particularly those of the family, of government and of religion. Riesman suspected that most people would not be "pure types" (although a person might be predominantly inner-directed, for example, she might also show some characteristics of the other types) and that most people adjust to their culture with varying degrees of success. Some people would be well-adjusted (adjustment), some would not (anomie), and some would transcend (autonomy). Using Riesman's three types of social character as one variable and adjustment success as the other, Stephenson created the following structured sample design:

	SOCIAL CHARACTER		
Adjustment-	Tradition	Inner	Other
Adjusted			
Anomie			
Autonomous			

The design calls for a "set" of 9 items (3 x 3) to be replicated as many times as desired. Each item would be classified as either Tradition, Inner or Other Directed and as either Adjusted, Anomie or Autonomous. The items were statements. Using Riesman's well-defined social-type characteristics, developed through extensive interviews, Stephenson asked people to describe themselves in the context of their social

Selecting P Samples

The selection of P (Persons) Samples is by far the easier of the two sampling procedures in Q Methodology. The procedures follow pretty much the same lines as those used in most social science research. Moreover, most of us are conceptually comfortable with the idea of sampling persons. The sampling of content--the concern in Q sampling--is new ground for most people and, consequently, more difficult to conceptualize.

P sampling is, like Q sampling, anchored by Fisherian experimental design principles and small sample doctrine. The goal is to select the sample with attention to known characteristics of individuals.

Suppose we are interested in studying attitudes about mandatory retirement. What demographic variables would you suspect might be related to how people think about mandatory retirement? Age should come immediately to mind. Someone close to retirement age is very likely to have strong attitudes about such matters. Quite young workers, conversely, may strongly resent the larger payroll checks taken home by their elderly colleagures and feel blocked in their efforts to gain promotions. Other variables might include income, education, occupation, union membership and so forth. Let's take three--age, income and occupation--and present them formally in the design below:

table

variable	levels
Age	a. 18-35 b. 36-50 c. 51-60 d. 61+
Income	a. 0-10,000 b. 10,001-18,000 c. 18,001+
Occupation	a. Prof/man. b. white collar c. blue collar

The variables selected need to be relevant--not merely any demographic variable one happens to think of and the levels, or subcategories, should be determined through careful thought. Usually, both variables and levels will be suggested by either the special demands of the study or as a direct result of the literature review. For our purposes, there is no need to discuss the rationale behind the design.

The sampling design is quite straightforward and no doubt like many you have seen before. There are four levels of age and three each for income and occupation. Thus, there are 36 possible combinations (4 x 3 x 3) of the variables: for example, $Age_1 Income_1 Occupation_1$ through $Age_4 Income_3 Occupation_3$. The design is an example of what is known typically as a stratified sample. Its advantages are its high degree of control and precision and its assurance that persons with specific known characteristics will not be left out of the study. This latter point is worth additional explanation. Certain combinations (or

Level × level × level

cells) of the variables are more prevalent in the population than others. For example, the proportion of people in the population who are 61+, hold a Professional/Managerial position and who earn $10,000 or less surely is smaller than the proportion who are 36-50, hold blue collar jobs, and earn $10,001-18,000. There may be so few, in fact, that if a simple random sample were selected not one of them would be included. On the other hand, those in the $A_2I_2O_3$ combinations might well make up more than half of the sample.

Operationally, one can use a stratified sample in several ways. People can be assigned to cells "after the fact." That is, a simple random sample can be selected and people can then be assigned to cells. This, of course, does not insure that the cells will be equal, or that each cell will be represented. The sample can be selected proportionately. For example, the number of people in the population who "belong to" each cell can be determined or estimated (for example, with census data), the proportion of the population in each cell is then determined, and the sample is drawn accordingly. Thus, if 42 per cent of the population belonged to cell $A_2I_2O_2$, 42 per cent of the people in the sample would have to come from that cell. In Q Methodology, the approach usually is to use a balanced block design, which calls for equal numbers of persons to be sampled for each cell.

In the example, then, 36 people--one to a cell--are needed. Assuming that the variables included in the design are meant to be used later to help explain the results, we likely would not be satisfied with only one person to represent a cell. Therefore, we would replicate the design as many times as thought necessary. Each replication will require 36 persons. Obviously, even a few replications will drastically increase the sample size.* Large samples are not needed in Q, as will become clearer in later chapters, and may actually distort results at the factor analysis stage. Care should be taken in designing samples to limit both the number of levels and variables to only what is necessary.

The sampling of persons usually should be done randomly. The simplest procedure is to draw a simple random sample. As persons are selected they are assigned to cells. Once a cell is "filled"--the required number of persons is obtained--additional people selected who belong to that cell are simply discarded. The procedure is not very efficient--to "fill" all the cells it may be necessary eventually to draw several hundred additional names to find the one or two persons needed to complete the sample.

---

*"Replicate" means to repeat. Therefore, two replications logically would mean three "sets"--the original and two "copies." Unfortunately, the word is seldom used that way in research. Three replications would mean three sets; in the example, 36 x 3 = 108 subjects.

Stephenson normally would not select people randomly. For his purposes one representative of a cell is just as good as any other and randomization is of no concern.

There are good reasons for random selection. Most statistical tests require random sampling, or an approximation to it. The use of statistics in Q does not follow "normal" lines, as might be expected of a methodology that deals with intraindividual significances instead of interindividual differences. Nonetheless, there is no good reason not to randomize. Random sampling takes the selection out of the hands of the investigator and helps eliminate all sorts of potential bias. For those new to research, the pitfalls are many and random selection can help the unwary be more surefooted.

Random sampling becomes considerably more difficult when a "Thompson schemata" is used. Thompson suggested that opinions could best be evaluated by systematically sampling persons likely to have different levels of interest in the topic. He identified five groups of people: (1) those likely to have special interest in the subject; (2) those who, given all the facts, could form a dispassionate opinion, as judges and jury-members are supposed to do; (3) those who are the existing "authorities" or experts on the topic; (4) those with class interests; and (5) those who are largely uninformed or uninterested in the topic. In a study of attitudes about movie ratings (GP, X, R, etc.), Yeager[2] used the Thompson schemata to produce this sampling design: (1) special interests--movie distributors, theater managers, juvenile authorities; (2) dispassionate interests--grade school and high school teachers; (3) authorities--those who have studied the effects of movies on children, including sociologists, psychologists, criminologists; (4) class interests--parents, teenagers, representatives of religious groups; (5) uninformed interests--members of the general public not included in other categories.

The Thompson approach is useful for Q studies because it systematically leads to the inclusion of people who are likely to look at a problem from very different viewpoints. We are not interested in direction--that is, whether people agree or disagree that the movie ratings are functionally useful. In fact, within any interest category we would expect to find people at different attitudinal "poles." Rather, the concern is with what dimensions are used by different people to evaluate the topic. People with special interests likely will use different "yardsticks" to measure a topic than will people with class interests. For example, a theater manager may evaluate the ratings in terms of economics (will R-rated movies attract as many customers, even at a higher price, as G-rated movies and which will produce greater

Some general suggestions:

1. Try to get a quick, general impression of what each factor is all about. This is best done by studying each factor's array, with particular attention to those statements with standard scores of greater than ± 1.00. Jot down notes and ideas.

2. When you think you've got a working handle on a factor, but you're still having trouble on the others, start comparing it with other factors--see how it differs, how it is alike, etc.

3. Put the Q arrays aside and study the extreme comments, and glance at the demographic variable breakdowns for some clues.

4. Always keep in mind that it matters little where any individual item is ranked. What is of concern is the overall pattern of the items and the rankings of combinations of items.

5. It is frequently useful to assign names to the factors. This, once again, tends to humanize the hypothetical entity and makes for much easier reading. For a particularly good example of factor naming, see Charles Mauldin thesis. Such names should accurately describe the factor. A danger is that the name can easily become more than just a useful descriptive label. Mauldin suggests, wisely I think, that factor names should be positive; that is, they should be names that people on the factor would not object to; indeed, they might say, "that's me."

6. Be on the alert for "double negatives," a negative item that has been sorted on the negative end of the continuum. Two negatives, of course, make a positive. For example, consider that the following statement was given a -2.00 by Factor III: "I dislike the concept of peer evaluation." The continuum is Most Disagree to Most Agree. Factor III strongly disagrees with the statement, indicating that he agrees with the oppositive of the statement (or, "I like the concept of peer evaluation").

concession sales?) and enforcement (how do I keep under-aged kids out of an R-rated movie?). Parents of young teenagers, on the other hand, are likely to think of the ratings in terms of what kinds of movies their children see and how they will be influenced by them. The topic is the same--movie ratings--and the direction may even be the same--both the manager and the parent dislike the system--but the reasons for liking or disliking are altogether different.

One could proceed to draw a Thompson-type sample in much the same manner as the stratified or structured sample. That is, select names at random, make preliminary contact and ask enough questions to determine which interest group the person belongs, assigning the person to a cell and continuing until all cels are filled. That approach, once you think about it, will be even more inefficient than it was for the other sampling design. In any given community there will be, for example, very few theater managers and the likelihood of selecting one of them randomly is so slight that it virtually can be eliminated as a possibility. Obviously it would make far greater sense to combine sampling methods. Thus, for easily identifiable groups--such as theater managers--a "list" would be made and a random sample could be selected. A check of the yellow pages in the telephone directory will indicate how many theaters there are and a phone call to each will identify the

managers. But where do you find experts or authorities? You will find no listing for "Experts on Movie Ratings" in the yellow pages. To determine through an interview whether someone is expert or not may be extremely time-consuming and inaccurate. Checking with persons with special interests may provide some leads. For a variety of topics, the best bet is likely to be a local college or university. Regarding a matter like movie ratings, it would be an unusual campus that would not have an authority to be found in the departments of sociology, psychology, journalism, mass communication, or speech. If they don't have an authority, someone on campus probably will be able to direct you to someone who is.

For many sampling requirements it will be best to follow the random sampling procedure. For others, however, it will be far better to forego random sampling and deliberately search out people with hard-to-find characteristics. Once a group of such people has been found, a random sample can be taken from it--assuming you found enough people.

An interesting, and rather embarrassing, example should drive the point home. As part of a semester-long project in a research methods course, the class had to produce a sampling design. The theory, long-since forgotten, deliberately was made complex. It required an

Variance Analysis of Structured Samples

The primary reason for developing structured Q samples is to use the structure as an aid in organizing items and as a means of providing clues for the interpretation of Q factors. The use of variance analysis with structured samples is, however, commonplace and it will be beneficial to discuss the problems involved while the nature of structured samples is fresh in the reader's mind.

Variance analysis in Q Methodology typically is used in two ways: to see how the variables built into the structured sample are dealt with by a given person, that is, intraindividually; and, to see how the variables are dealt with by Q factors (or types). Thus, a person can be given a structured sample of items and asked to complete a Q sort and the data provided can be submitted to analysis of variance. The Q array for any factor can be analyzed likewise.

In proceeding with such analyses, Stephenson relies heavily on the concepts of small-sample theory inherent in Fisherian experimental design.[1] Simplistically, the principle in Fisherian design is to provide a situation in which one or more variables are systematically varied and their effects (and interactive effects) are measured in relation to the amount of unexplained variance or error.

1. Fisher

Fisher's work provided the foundations for modern experimental research design. Traditionally, experimentation typically had proceeded laboriously to manipulate one variable at a time. Thus, in matters relating to agriculture, for example, it literally took years (or growing seasons) to determine optimum combinations of seed corn, fertilizer, and the like. Statistical analysis, for the most part, dealt with the problem of error variance through the law of large numbers. Galton's description is apt: "...whenever a large sample of chaotic elements are taken in hand and marshalled in the order of their magnitude, an unsuspected and most beautiful form of regularity proves to have been latent all the time."[2] In other words, out of chaos comes order, if large enough numbers or cases are gathered. Statistically, as the sample size increases, error decreases. Large sampling, consequently, was the primary means of controlling error and the effects of unidentified or apparently uncontrollable variables.

Fisherian design opened the avenues for simultaneous, multiple treatments (manipulations) and made possible the study of the interactions between them. Rather than relying on large samples to bring order out of chaos, extraneous systematic variance (i.e., from contaminating variables) could be controlled directly by incorporating them into the design--a vastly more efficient procedure.[3] Moreover,

2. Galton, see Play, p17
3. Lindquist says it is better not to randomize if you don't have to.

the need to minimize error variance was eliminated by partitioning error variance into component parts and using a more precise error estimate as the denominator in the well-known F ratio. In other words, Fisherian design takes whatever error variance is present, measures it, and compares it to the variance associated with the independent variables. How much error is present, thus, is not important so long as the explained variance is proportionately greater. Thus, Fisherian methodology can proceed by way of small samples. Large samples are not needed to reduce error. Order comes out of chaos through the provision of greater variable control, more precise estimates, and the use of the ratio, explained to unexplained variance.

Using Fisher's design principles, Stephenson structures Q samples according to some relevant theory. An item is selected or created to fit each cell of a balanced block design. The design is replicated n times and the replication variance is tested for homogeneity. "In general, if the data are proved homogeneous at the point of replications, we may suppose that the principle or randomization has operated adequately during the person's self-description and that contingencies are not involved where they were not expected.⁴ Small sample theory, with its concern for rigorous exercise of variables, is fundamental.

4. Stephenson, ibid., p. 93.

The use of analysis of variance on Q data has been criticized by several investigators.⁵ The major criticisms seem to be: (1) items, and hence their scores, are not randomly selected from an infinite population; (2) item ratings are not independent of each other--that is, the rank-ordering procedure requires that items be considered relative to each other; (3) when a forced distribution system is used, each person's mean (elevation) and standard deviation (scatter) are the same. Stephenson anticipated such criticisms and consequently dealt with them in The Study of Behavior. It is beyond the scope of this book to deal at length with some of the complex issues already covered by Stephenson. We would, however, like to make several observations that should shed some light on statistical matters.

Most criticisms of variance analysis of Q data stem from confusion about the purpose of such analysis or from an unwillingness to accept premise Stephenson believes fundamental. From Stephenson's viewpoint, many of the statistical criticisms are non sequitors.

For example, a frequent criticism is that the statistical limitations inherent in the method make it inappropriate to generalize the results of analysis of variance to parent populations. Such generalizations are not at issue in Q methodology, as Stephenson has taken pains to explain repeatedly. Another frequent criticism is that Q

Methodology lacks proper normative underpinnings. By now you well know that Q deals with matters ipsative (of the self) rather than with matters normative. The classic non sequitor, however, is that "Q Methodology seems to defy all principles of deductive logic."[6] Exactly Stephenson's concern, of course, is with abduction and inductive inferences.

Some of the criticisms may stem from confusion about how Stephenson uses analysis of variance. He does not use it normatively, to generalize to parent populations, but to assist in the explanation of factors. Some confusion may exist for those who think Fisherian experimental design "means" analysis of variance. Stephenson uses Fisher's principles of design but opts for a different mode (factor analysis) to analyze the data. Analysis of variance is but an aid. The issues involved in design are not the same as those in analysis. "The science of data analysis (Tukey, 1962) is closely tied to the real world. Its purpose is to derive certain conclusions about the 'state of the world' from a sample of evidence. Statistics, on the other hand, is a mathematical discipline and can't be evaluated by the same empirical considerations. Consequently, although data analysis finds statistics very useful, it is helpful to maintain a distinction."[7]

6.

7. Graes and Luckar, quoting Tukey, p.311.

Compared with Q methodology, R's sampling of tests or stimuli, if not small, is preconceived: In R, for example, "operational definitions and validity are prerequisite since...a standard meaning from person to person" must "be assumed for a test," or the finding that "individual a has a higher score than b on scale X," has no meaning (p. 174). Therefore, R's "rating scales, like thermometers, must have a priori meaning. That, "in turn, necessitates large numbers of cases, since only in this way can it be safely assumed that private meanings have canceled out in the long run, leaving the arithmetic average as an expression of 'true meaning' (within error)" (p. 174). It rests on differential psychology, for "differences in scores between subhjects are assumed to reflect individual differences in the amount of the variable contained by persons."

In contrast, Q is based on "intraindividual differences in significance," for "differences in scores between sample elements (statements) are assumed to reflect differences in the amount of importance attributed to them by the person....Operant responses, rather than operational definitions, are at issue. The concept of [external] validity has very little status" since we have "no outside criterion for a person's own point of view." However, internal validity is important. The subject might be deceiving the researcher--or himself. Consequently, researchers try to alter the conditions of instruction "to induce the subject to 'give himself away' or [to] otherwise reveal other operants than those of which he is aware" (pp. 174-175). Consequently, general meanings for the items are "apprehended a posteriori."

◼ 이제영

서울 배재고등학교 졸업
한국외국어대학교 인도어과 문학사
한국외국어대학교 대학원 신문방송학과 정치학 석사
한국외국어대학교 대학원 신문방송학과 정치학 박사
현) 한국광고PR실학회 총무이사
현) 한국콘텐츠학회 논문지편집이사 및 편집위원
현) 한국언론학회 편집위원
현) 가톨릭관동대학교 광고홍보학과 교수
저서) 방송규제와 공영성, 신문산업론, 중국의 광고산업,
 녹색건강산업 광고매체론, 미디어와 주관성,
 커뮤니케이션과 미디어, 정치인과 홍보이미지 외 다수.

Q의 의미

▶
초 판 인 쇄 | 2016년 12월 26일
초 판 발 행 | 2016년 12월 29일
저　　　자 | 이 제 영
펴　낸　이 | 권 호 순
펴　낸　곳 | 시간의물레
▶
등　　　록 | 2004년 6월 5일
주　　　소 | (121-050)서울시 마포구 마포대로 4다길 3, 1층
전　　　화 | (02)3273-3867
팩　　　스 | (02)3273-3868
전자우편 | timeofr@naver.com
블 로 그 | http://blog.naver.com/mulretime
홈페이지 | http://www.mulretime.com
▶ ISBN 978-89-6511-173-3 (93300)
정가 9,800원
ⓒ 이제영 2016

* 이 책의 저작권은 저자에게 출판권은 시간의물레에 있습니다.
* 잘못 만들어진 책은 교환해드립니다.